INSTANT POT MINI COOKBOOK 3 QUART

Instant Pot Mini Cookbook 3 Quart

100 Amazing Recipes for 3 Quart Instant Pot Mini Duo

Kristy Asai

LEGAL NOTICE

Copyright (c) 2019 by Kristy Asai

All rights are reserved. No portion of this book may be reproduced or duplicated using any form whether mechanical, electronic, or otherwise. No portion of this book may be transmitted, stored in a retrieval database, or otherwise made available in any manner whether public or private unless specific permission is granted by the publisher. Vector illustration credit: vecteezy.com

This book does not offer advice, but merely provides information. The author offers no advice whether medical, financial, legal, or otherwise, nor does the author encourage any person to pursue any specific course of action discussed in this book. This book is not a substitute for professional advice. The reader accepts complete and sole responsibility for the manner in which this book and its contents are used. The publisher and the author will not be held liable for any damages caused.

CONTENTS

INTRODUCTION TO THE INSTANT POT MINI 7

POULTRY RECIPES 17

PORK RECIPES 41

BEEF RECIPES 65

SEAFOOD RECIPES 89

VEGETABLE RECIPES 111

THE "DIRTY DOZEN" AND "CLEAN 15" 126

MEASUREMENT CONVERSION TABLES 127

INDEX 128

INTRODUCTION TO THE INSTANT POT MINI

The most important thing for any household is to have products that will help them to live a better life. That is the whole point of technology and why we are constantly trying hard to improve it, and to make sure that every new year is stronger and full of brand new technology. We have the talent to take ordinary things and to turn them into extraordinary appliances, which will bring a revolution to the houses and the families that use them.

The same is true for the humble pot. What was once simply a utensil in the kitchen, which was used for hours to make delicious meals, has now become a complex symbol of technology. We have gone beyond the simple pot, and have replaced it with the wonderful instant pot! An appliance that makes life easier, cheaper, and far more convenient in the kitchen than ever before.

The instant pot dates back to the 17th century, when it was first invented as a simple steam machine, with the aim of speeding up the process of cooking meat and vegetables. It worked wonders, and since then, it has constantly been improved and adapted to fulfill the needs of modern society. We now have different varieties of these cookers, and each one has its very own special features, and things that it does better than others.

WHY YOU SHOULD USE AN INSTANT POT

The instant pot's purpose is to cook food under high pressure. This effectively means that it can drastically reduce the cooking time of the ingredients, without ruining their nutritional properties. This is an absolutely revolution for families, who have a difficult time balancing between work and taking care of their children and themselves.

Because we no longer live in a traditional environment where one parent is always at home and the other one works short hours, people have had to find other ways to make their lives easier, and also, more affordable. Because the instant pot uses the high power of pressure to cook food, it can, for example, prepare a stew that would usually take 90 minutes in just 40. It can also easily break down lean meats and starchy vegetables, without the cook worrying about their ingredients overcooking or undercooking.

These appliances have also been technologically improved to fit every household, to be safe, and to have all the right settings so that they can provide the most delicious food possible, for a much lower price. When you have the option of combining any kind of food together, and creating delicious meals out of anything, it suddenly becomes much easier to control your budget, and to purchase products that suit your needs best. This is why so many families have switched to an instant pot when it comes to deciding on what to cook for the day.

But perhaps one of the most impressive products that has entered the market is the amazing Instant Pot Mini! It provides families and households with everything they need from a pressure cooker, but at the best possible size and with all the right settings. Let's find out more about how this wonderful little appliance can make you fall in love with cooking all over again!

An Overview of the Instant Pot Mini

Unlike what you would usually expect from large pressure cookers, this appliance is a smaller size, but packs the same amount of power and punch to every meal! What makes it so great is that it fits into a kitchen of any size, and it doesn't mess with the initial look of the home. This is often very important for families, because they have a specific design for their home and how they want their kitchens to function, so if something disturbs that peace with its massive size, it will likely become an appliance that isn't used very often.

This is of course not the case with the Instant Pot Mini. And yet, one of the things that makes it so impressive is its advanced ability to cook delicious meals from almost any ingredient imaginable. There are of course delicious recipes that can be followed for the Instant Pot Mini, but you can also easily get creative with your own favorite ingredients, as long as you make sure to follow the manufacturer's advice on how to use the appliance.

There really are no limits to the things that can be cooked inside the Instant Pot Mini, which means that you don't need to bring a complex shopping list when you head on over to the grocery store. The best rule of thumb is to look for ingredients that are of similar density, because it means that they will likely take a similar amount of time to cook, which means that they are perfect for being combined together. For example, you can combine leans meats with potatoes and root vegetables, because they will roughly take the same amount of time to cook. Likewise, you can also combine fish with leafy greens, because they too are of similar density, hence will take a similar time to cook.

But perhaps even more importantly for families is the fact that this instant pot is wonderful for the family budget. Food is usually the thing that we all spend most of our income on, so whenever there is something that can help us save money on it, it is always wonderful news. Because you can use ingredients that are often difficult to cook the traditional way, and yet are also cheaper, there is no end to how creative you can now become in the kitchen, without worrying about what it will mean for your finances. This is just one of many things that have separated the Instant Pot Mini from so many other appliances!

The Best Features of the Instant Pot Mini

Although it may look like just one appliance, the Instant Pot Mini is in fact a number of different appliances combined together! It acts as a Pressure Cooker, Slow Cooker, Rice Cooker, Steamer, Sauté, Yogurt Maker, Sterilizer and Warmer! There is almost nothing that this humble kitchen appliance cannot prepare, which is exactly what makes it so unique, and why it is such a wonderful investment for a family home.

There are a few different designs to choose from, as well as a slight difference between them, but they are all wonderful additions to any kitchen and will help immensely with anything that has to do with efficient, healthy eating. It's also very easy to store away too if you don't wish to use it for a while.

The great thing about this appliance is that it does so many things on its own, without any need for outside human interference. This includes both the cooking procedures and the safety procedures as well. Inside is an embedded microprocessor which monitors every aspect of the appliance.

Everything from the temperature, pressure, and time, to adjusting its own heating, and even switching off on its own if the pressure reaches dangerous levels. This is very unlikely to happen of course, but it is great to know that the appliance is capable of handling itself, especially in homes that have pets and children who may spend time close to the appliance without adult supervision.

The Instant Pot Mini's main goal is to produce food that is of the highest quality, regardless of the ingredients that have ben chosen to go inside it. Its manual describes in great detail which settings are best for each ingredient, which means that all you have to do is follow that manual and you will always come away with a delicious meal.

Here are some of the best features that come with the Instant Pot Mini! There are plenty more to choose from, but we will highlight these because they are especially good in making life that much more delicious and easy.

24-hour delay in cooking

Imagine being able to plan tomorrow's meal an entire day in advance? Well now you can, because the Instant Pot Mini has a timer which allows you to prep all the ingredients the day before, and then start the cook on the following day. This has been a remarkable help for the main cooks of the house, because they no longer have to worry about tomorrow's meals. This setting works best with meat and vegetables, although it can also be used with a few other ingredients.

Your food kept constantly warm

The Instant Pot Mini can keep food warm for many hours, which is also a great addition for people who love to plan their meals in advance. There is nothing better than coming home from work and having an entire, warm meal already waiting for you. Additionally, you can also use this option if you intend to eat the same meal again later on in the day, or even if you'd like to use it as a leftover for tomorrow.

Full flavors regardless of the ingredients

Pressure cookers sometimes get a bad rap for, supposedly, causing the food to lose its flavor once the cooking process is over. However, this is not the case with the Instant Pot Mini. If anything, because it is made with the perfect sealed environment in mind, it actually traps all the flavors and sends them back down to the food. Traditional cooking methods would cause the flavors to evaporate, but this is not the case with this handy appliance. Which means that you can enjoy any meals of your choice without worrying at all about what it will taste like.

No burnt food

The stainless steel bottom of the Instant Pot Mini protect all the food from the possibility of burning. Not only is this great for the actual meal, but more importantly, it also means that you don't have to worry about the negative health side effects of burnt food. If consumed for long periods of time, it brings in too many toxins into the human body, which is why burnt food is so often related to causes of cancer. But with the Instant Pot Mini there is nothing to worry about, because the pot takes care of itself and does all the work.

Cool accessories come with the Instant Pot Mini

When you purchase this appliance, you will be gifted with some very useful accessories, which you can use in your everyday cooking. The accessories include a recipe book, a soup spoon, a condensation collector, a measuring cup, a rice paddle, and a stainless steel steam rack without handles. This is great for getting you started right away, so that you don't have to worry about purchasing any additional things before you actually start cooking. And, they are also very easy to clean because they are made from the same quality materials.

Perhaps its most impressive feature – the safety mechanisms

High pressure and high temperatures are enough to make people afraid of using an appliance, especially if there are children running around the house. However, the Instant Pot Mini creators have gone above and beyond to ensure that every single safety mechanism has been applied and is working properly, which almost certainly guarantees that the appliance will continue to work without any problems and that there is nothing that either parents or children should be afraid of. Of course, the best way to go about this is to make sure that you are always following the manufacturer's instructions when using the appliance, because the instructions have been designed specifically for safety purposes, to ensure that no one is ever hurt when using an instant pot.

It has no less than 10 different safety mechanisms to keep everything in check. It has also been certified by UL & ULC, which means that all of these 10 safety features have a specific, high safety purpose on the appliance.

For example, it has a number of different **pressure regulators**, which make sure that the pressure which is building inside the pot is not going to any extreme levels that cannot be controlled. As long as the user is following the instructions this is almost impossible to happen, but just in case, the manufacturer has installed a feature where the Instant Pot Mini will turn off on its own if it senses that the pressure might be going out of control. This is a huge step from previous pressure cookers, where people would have to judge by eye how high the pressure has gotten, and then also decide on their own when it's time to release the pressure.

The **anti-blockage vent** prevents any food debris from blocking the vent. This would cause very bad smells to accumulate over time, and it also used to be very difficult to clean and collect this food debris. However, it had now been controlled and change to a much easier way of handling this situation. The vent needs to be clear at all times because it is where the pressure will shoot out from once the pressure cooker is done with its work. If the vent isn't clean, the pressure actually bend the cooker into an odd shape, or in the worst case scenario, it could also cause the lid to blow off. However, there is no reason to worry about such things with the Instant Pot Mini, because it does all of this hard work on its own and makes sure that the user will feel safe at all times while using the appliance.

Speaking of which, the Instant Pot Mini also has a **safety lid lock**, which prevents the lid from opening by accident at any point of the cook. This is a very important feature for two reasons. The first, and less dangerous, one is because an open lid is not able to accumulate any pressure, or the right temperature, in order to properly cook the food. The second, and much more dangerous reason, is because if the lid is loose and the pressure starts to build up too much, the lid could suddenly come off and cause damage or a mess in the kitchen. With this special safety feature, this is no longer a problem for any home cooks.

Additionally, it also has a **sensor for lid position detection**, which means that it monitors how securely the lid has been locked, or if it has been locked at all. If there are any problems, the appliance will alert the user right away, and will therefore prevent any future accident from happening. This is also important because there are times when people do not place the Instant Pot Mini in a safe position on a regular counter, but instead choose to place it in place that were not meant for cooking, or at a weird angle. This safety feature alerts if any of these mistakes have been made, and easily reminds the user that they should be fixed before any further damage is made.

The **automatic temperature control** feature ensures that the temperature inside the instant pot is always monitored to be at the perfect temperature for the type of meal that is being prepared. If for whatever reason the temperature drops or goes up too high, the appliance will regulate itself and bring the temperature back to the ideal number. This is a great feature because it allows the food to be coked perfectly and without any worries of over or under cooking the food.

Pressure protection makes sure that the pressure inside the cooker is always kept at the optimal levels, and will never be able to go up too high to dangerous numbers. This is what usually makes people so afraid of pressure cookers, this idea that it will at some moment just decide to blow up if it hasn't been set to work properly. This is, for all pressure cookers, a very unlikely event. However, there is nothing wrong with going the extra mile when it comes to safety features, making sure that this doesn't happen in your case, or in anyone else's.

In order to prevent this specific problem from ever happening, the Instant Pot Mini also has an **electrical current and temperature fuse**, which will cut off all the power if it deems that it needs to do so in order to prevent a dangerous situation from happening. This means that all users can rest assured that, even if they leave the instant pot alone for a while, it will be able to take care of itself and will keep the house and everyone in it safe for as long as needed.

Just a Few Negative Things About the Instant Pot Mini

There is no such thing as a perfect appliance, and the case is the same with the Instant Pot Mini. There are a few things that are not so great about it, although this doesn't mean that they cannot be learned or fixed. However, in the hope of being objective at all times we must mention everything that has to do with the negative parts of the Instant Pot Mini.

Despite how great the instructions might be, some people are still afraid of the pressure cooker, even one as cute as Instant Pot Mini – It makes sense that people are distrusting of things that they've never tried before, especially things that have to do with high pressure and high temperature. However, pressure cookers have been so well developed over the years that there really is absolutely nothing to worry about when it comes to using them. Instead of worrying about what will happen should you use one, it is a much better idea to think of all the positive things that will come with it.

You need to learn the settings properly and also the order of ingredients that go into the Instant Pot Mini. - Like all pressure cookers, this one is also based on the understanding that once you start the pressure cooker you will not be touching it again until the food is officially done. However, different ingredients require different cooking times, so it really is important to understand your ingredients and to combine the ones that have similar cooking times as often as possible. There are of course opportunities to stop the pressure cooker and then open in half-way through a cook to add a different ingredient, but it often defeats the purpose of a pressure cooker in the first place. Instead, focus on combining ingredients that won't have you worried about their cooking times.

VERSIONS OF THE INSTANT POT MINI

With a few small differences, all variations of the Instant Pot Mini are a wonderful appliance to add to a household, and will serve you with delicious food for years to come. They are also all great for cooking food for all dietary preferences, so it doesn't matter which ingredients you use in your kitchen, they will all become the best versions of themselves as soon as they enter the pressure cooker.

However, one of the reasons why people choose the 'mini' version rather than the regular-sized pressure cookers is because of comfort. It could, of course, also be because they realize that they may not need such a huge pot for their everyday cooking, this is especially true for smaller families, or for those who are planning on using the pressure cooker for its very specific features. But that's not the only reason why going mini in size may actually be a great choice on a number of different levels. Let's discuss some of them below.

Very easy to use

Because of their size, the mini instant pot are not as intimidating as the regular large ones, which means that they are a great introduction to pressure cooking for people who have never used such an appliance before. You'd be surprised how many people have never even used an electric pot, simply because they preferred to stick to traditional methods of cooking. However, as soon as the Instant Pot Mini is brought to the home, it only takes a few minutes to go through the instructions and to start cooking.

Also, and this is also because of its size, users find it much easier to calculate the right amount of liquid to put inside the pressure cooker when they first start using it. Many people overdo the liquid, which can be dangerous (although the safety mechanisms in the Instant Pot Mini would warn the user). But the bottom line is that liquid really is a problem, both because it can overflow once it starts boiling, but also because if the user puts too little of it, the food will not have enough liquid to cook in.

Another wonderful feature of the mini editions is that they can fit *anywhere*. Most people may instantly think that they would just use them in their kitchen, but did you know that they are also great in dorm rooms and boats? You could also take it camping! Remember that one of the most important things about the pressure cooker is that it create delicious meals, at half the time, and frequently at half the price as well. This is why it is so versatile in where it can be taken, and why even students can really make the most of it at university, so that they can ensure that they are having proper meals and not just fast food. Although most people wouldn't think of it in this use, this simple appliance could easily make so many lives that much easier.

How to Properly Clean the Instant Pot Mini

Regardless of how great an appliance may be, the only way to truly make sure that you are using it to its best potential is to make sure that you are maintaining it the way that it should be done so. There are of course instructions in the manual that will help you with this process, but there are also some common sense instructions that you should really take note of when you are using a pressure cooker, and the Instant Pot Mini is no different.

Taking care of the appliance s super easy, especially because of its stainless steel material, which makes it easy to remove food and prevents it from both burning and sticking. But you need to also understand the tools that you should use when you want to clean you Instant Pot Mini and have it ready next use. Remember, it doesn't matter how great an appliance has been designed, whenever you are working with food, you need to make sure that everything is in order so as to prevent any mold from forming on any bacteria from spreading.

Never keep the appliance plugged in before you start cleaning it – Regardless of how well the appliance may have been made, never keep it plugged into a wall if you are attempting to clean it. Anything that has to do with a combination of water and electricity is never a good idea, so make sure to always keep it away from electricity until it is completely dry. If you think that you may have done anything to the appliance to make it too wet to use, contact the manufacturer immediately before trying to do anything on your own when it comes to cleaning it.

Take your time and make sure that everything has been cleaned properly – Do not just skim over the appliance when cleaning it. Instead, make sure that you are doing your best to really reach every single crack of the appliance. Food is a sensitive thing to deal with, and if left alone, it really loves to grow its own moss and bacteria. However, you certainly don't want this to happen for yourself or for anyone in your family, so it's best to make sure that everything is cleaned to perfection before your next use.

Make sure that the pressure valve is always clean – As we mentioned a little earlier, the valve is very important for the moment when that pressure that's been building up needs to be released. In order to ensure that everything goes as it should, make sure to take just a little extra time to clean the valve.

Warm water and the right shampoo are enough for cleaning the Instant Pot Mini – because it is made of stainless steel, it really doesn't take much to clean the entire instant pot and make it nice and shiny again. Never use abrasive cleaners for your instant pot. Any regular kitchen shampoo is all you need, and some warm water. If you feel that the food has left a stronger mark on the top than you'd like to see, you can always soak the cooking part of the pot for about an hour and then clean it. The reason why it is so important to not destroy the stainless steel base is because it will have a huge effect on your food and may be dangerous because it can no longer maintain heat properly throughout.

If you still feel that you may need to clean the outside of the appliance, do it with care – It is very important that you take special care if you need to clean the outside of the appliance, the part where there are switches, cords, and screens. You can do this with a damp cloth, and make sure that it is not too soaked because you may no longer be able to understand where the water has gone.

Also, there may also be a danger of the switches and the electrical parts of the appliances becoming too wet. If you think that you may have made a mistake, contact your manufacturer and see if there is anything they can do to help you out. It's always better to get an expert in, rather than trying to do something on your own and do it badly.

A Wonderful Appliance Fit for Any Lifestyle

The Instant Pot Mini is a mini revolution when it comes to pressure cookers and their technology. It has brought the best of the traditional instant pot, but in a smaller, much more manageable size. Many people are now enjoying an easier and healthier life because of it, and they were able to add it to their lifestyle without too much trouble at all.

And, with its different varieties and styles, you now also have the option of choosing the one that suits you most and fits your budget best. The best way to go about it is to take some time to go through the slight differences between the appliances, and to choose the one that will truly fit yourself and your family best!

POULTRY RECIPES

Contents

Creamy Chicken Soup 18
Chicken & Kale Soup 19
Chicken & Squash Soup 20
Chicken & Chickpeas Soup 21
Creamy Chicken Stew 22
Chicken & Mushroom Stew 23
Chicken, Rice & Lentil Stew 24
Chicken & Veggie Chili 25
Chicken & Corn Chili 26
Chicken & Tomato Curry 27
Chicken & Veggie Curry 28
Sweet & Sour Shredded Chicken 29
Creamy Shredded Chicken 30
Chicken with Pineapple 31
Chicken with Olives 32
Chicken with Salsa 33
Herbed Chicken Breasts 34
Spicy Chicken Thighs 35
Sweet & Sour Chicken Thighs 36
Roasted Whole Chicken 37
Turkey with Quinoa & Chickpeas 38
Turkey Stuffed Bell Peppers 39

Creamy Chicken Soup

Serves: 4 / Preparation time: 15 minutes / Cooking time: 40 minutes

2 (6-ounce) skinless, boneless chicken breasts

4 cups chicken broth, divided

2 tablespoons canola oil

2 large onions, chopped

2 jalapeño peppers, chopped

2 garlic cloves, minced

5 cups tomatoes, chopped

1½ cups heavy cream

Salt and ground black pepper, to taste

1 cup fresh cilantro, chopped

- In the pot of Instant Pot Mini, place the chicken breast and ½ cup of broth.
- Secure the lid and turn to "Seal" position.
- Cook on "Manual" with "High Pressure" for about 20 minutes.
- Press the "Cancel" and allow a "Natural" release.
- Carefully, remove the lid and transfer the breasts into a bowl.
- Set aside to cool completely.
- Add the oil in an Instant Pot Mini and select "Sauté". Now, add the onion and cook for about 3-4 minutes.
- Add the jalapeño peppers and garlic and cook for about 1 minute.
- Add the tomatoes and cook for about 2 minutes.
- Press the "Cancel" and let the tomato mixture cool.
- In a food processor, add tomato mixture and pulse until smooth.
- In the pot, add the tomato mixture and remaining broth and stir to combine.
- Secure the lid and turn to "Seal" position.
- Cook on "Manual" with "High Pressure" for about 10 minutes.
- Press the "Cancel" and allow a "Natural" release.
- Meanwhile, with 2 forks, shred the chicken breasts.
- Carefully, remove the lid and select "Sauté".
- Stir in the shredded chicken, cream, salt, black pepper and cook for about 2-3 minutes.
- Press the "Cancel" and serve hot.

Per Serving: Calories: 438; Total Fat: 28.7g; Saturated Fat: 12.5g; Protein: 27.9g; Carbs: 19.1g; Fiber: 4.7g; Sugar: 10.1g

Chicken & Kale Soup

Serves: 4 / Preparation time: 15 minutes / Cooking time: 12 minutes

2 tablespoons olive oil

2 carrots, peeled and chopped

½ teaspoon dried oregano, crushed

4 cups chicken broth

¾ pound cooked chicken, shredded

½ teaspoon Worcestershire sauce

2 celery stalks, chopped

1 medium onion, chopped

Salt and ground black pepper, to taste

1 cup water

2 cups fresh kale, trimmed and chopped

- Add the oil in an Instant Pot Mini and select "Sauté". Now, add the celery, carrot and onion and cook for about 5 minutes.
- Add the herbs and black pepper and cook for about 1 minute.
- Press the "Cancel" and stir in the broth and water.
- Secure the lid and turn to "Seal" position.
- Select "Soup" and just use the default time of 4 minutes.
- Press the "Cancel" and allow a "Quick" release.
- Carefully, remove the lid and mix in the chicken and kale.
- Select "Sauté" and cook for about 1-2 minutes more.
- Press the "Cancel" and stir in the Worcestershire sauce.
- Serve immediately.

Per Serving: Calories: 269; Total Fat: 11g; Saturated Fat: 2.1g; Protein: 31.3g; Carbs: 10.5g; Fiber: 2.1g; Sugar: 3.6g

Chicken & Squash Soup

Serves: 4 / Preparation time: 15 minutes / Cooking time: 21 minutes

1 tablespoon olive oil

¼ cup onion, chopped

¼ cup carrots, peeled and chopped

¼ cup celery, chopped

1 garlic clove, minced

½ teaspoon dried thyme, crushed

¾ pound cooked butternut squash, peeled and cubed

1 cup tomatoes, chopped finely

2½ cups chicken broth

Salt and ground black pepper, to taste

2 cups cooked chicken, cut into small pieces

½ cup scallion, sliced thinly

- Add the oil in an Instant Pot Mini and select "Sauté". Now, add the onion, chopped scallion, carrot and celery and cook for about 5 minutes.
- Add the garlic and thyme and cook for about 1 minute.
- Press the "Cancel" and stir in the squash, tomato, broth, salt and black pepper.
- Secure the lid and turn to "Seal" position.
- Cook on "Manual" with "High Pressure" for about 10 minutes.
- Press the "Cancel" and allow a "Quick" release.
- Carefully, remove the lid and mix in the chicken.
- Select "Sauté" and cook for about 4-5 minutes.
- Press the "Cancel" and serve with the topping of scallion slices.

Per Serving: Calories: 221; Total Fat: 6.7g; Saturated Fat: 1.4g; Protein: 25.2g; Carbs: 15.5g; Fiber: 3.2g; Sugar: 4.7g

Chicken & Chickpeas Soup

Serves: 4 / Preparation time: 15 minutes / Cooking time: 20 minutes

1 tablespoon olive oil

3 (4-ounce) skinless boneless chicken breasts, chopped

Salt and ground black pepper, as required

1 medium onion, chopped

2 garlic cloves, minced

½ teaspoon dried rosemary, crushed

1 medium sweet potato, peeled and cubed

1 cup tomatoes, chopped finely

2½ cups chicken broth

2 cups fresh spinach, chopped

1 cup canned chickpeas, rinsed and drained

- Add the oil in an Instant Pot Mini and select "Sauté". Now, add the chicken, salt and black pepper and cook for about 5 minutes or until browned.
- With a slotted spoon, transfer the chicken breasts onto a plate.
- In the pot, add the onion and cook for about 5 minutes.
- Add the garlic and rosemary and cook for about 1 minute.
- Press the "Cancel" and stir in the cooked chicken, sweet potatoes, tomatoes, broth and spinach.
- Secure the lid and turn to "Seal" position.
- Cook on "Manual" with "High Pressure" for about 4 minutes.
- Press the "Cancel" and allow a "Quick" release.
- Carefully, remove the lid and mix in the chickpeas.
- Select "Sauté" and cook for about 4-5 minutes.
- Press the "Cancel" and stir in the salt and black pepper.
- Serve hot.

Per Serving: Calories: 388; Total Fat: 8.7g; Saturated Fat: 1.1g; Protein: 40.5g; Carbs: 42.5g; Fiber: 11.3g; Sugar: 10.1g

Creamy Chicken Stew

Serves: 4 / Preparation time: 15 minutes / Cooking time: 12 minutes

For Sauce

1 ounce cashews

1 onion, chopped

½ Serrano pepper

1 teaspoon garam masala

½ teaspoon ground cumin

½ cup tomatoes, chopped

5 garlic cloves, chopped

1 teaspoon fresh ginger, chopped

½ teaspoon ground coriander

½ teaspoon red chili pepper

Salt, to taste

For Stew

1 pound chicken thighs

½ cup unsweetened coconut milk

¾ cup water

¼ cup fresh cilantro, chopped

- For sauce: in a blender, add all the ingredients and pulse until smooth.
- In the pot of Instant Pot Mini, add the chicken thighs and cashew sauce and stir to combine.
- Secure the lid and turn to "Seal" position.
- Cook on "Manual" with "High Pressure" for about 10 minutes.
- Press the "Cancel" and allow a "Natural" release.
- Carefully, remove the lid and with tongs, transfer the chicken thighs onto a cutting board.
- Cut the chicken thighs into bite size pieces.
- Now, select "Sauté" and stir in chicken pieces and coconut milk.
- Cook for about 1-2 minutes.
- Press the "Cancel" and serve hot with the garnishing of cilantro.

Per Serving: Calories: 349; Total Fat: 19.1g; Saturated Fat: 9.3g; Protein: 35.5g; Carbs: 9.3g; Fiber: 2g; Sugar: 3.3g

Chicken & Mushroom Stew

Serves: 4 / Preparation time: 15 minutes / Cooking time: 16 minutes

1 tablespoon olive oil

¾ pound fresh cremini mushrooms, stemmed and quartered

1 small onion, chopped

3 garlic cloves, minced

1 cup green olives, pitted and halved

½ cup chicken broth

¼ cup fresh parsley, chopped

1 tablespoon tomato paste

4 (5-ounce) skinless chicken thighs

1½ cups fresh cherry tomatoes

Salt and ground black pepper, to taste

- Add the oil in the Instant Pot and select "Sauté". Now, add the mushrooms and onion and cook for about 4-5 minutes.
- Stir in the tomato paste and garlic and cook for about 1 minute.
- Press the "Cancel" and stir in the chicken, olives, tomatoes and broth.
- Secure the lid and turn to "Seal" position.
- Cook on "Manual" with "High Pressure" for about 10 minutes.
- Press the "Cancel" and allow a "Quick" release.
- Carefully, remove the lid and mix in the salt, black pepper and parsley.
- Serve hot.

Per Serving: Calories: 393; Total Fat: 18.1g; Saturated Fat: 4g; Protein: 45.2g; Carbs: 11.7g; Fiber: 3.1g; Sugar: 4.6g

Chicken, Rice & Lentil Stew

Serves: 4 / Preparation time: 15 minutes / Cooking time: 16 minutes

2 tablespoons olive oil

2 (4-ounce) skinless, boneless chicken breasts

Salt and ground black pepper, as required

4 garlic cloves, minced

½ cup brown rice

½ cup dried lentils

1 sweet potato, peeled and cubed

1 russet potato, peeled and cubed

1 teaspoon ground coriander

1 teaspoon ground cumin

½ teaspoon ground coriander

1 teaspoon cayenne pepper

2 cups chicken broth

1½ cups water

- Add the oil in an Instant Pot Mini and select "Sauté". Now, add the chicken, salt and black pepper and cook for about 5 minutes or until browned.
- With a slotted spoon, transfer the chicken breasts onto a plate.
- In the pot, add the garlic and cook for about 1 minute.
- Press the "Cancel" and stir in the cooked chicken and remaining ingredients.
- Secure the lid and turn to "Seal" position.
- Cook on "Manual" with "High Pressure" for about 10 minutes.
- Press the "Cancel" and allow a "Quick" release.
- Carefully, remove the lid and serve hot.

Per Serving: Calories: 387; Total Fat: 10.9g; Saturated Fat: 2.2g; Protein: 24.8g; Carbs: 47.8g; Fiber: 10.3g; Sugar: 3.1g

Chicken & Veggie Chili

Serves: 4 / Preparation time: 15 minutes / Cooking time: 10 minutes

2 carrots, peeled and cubed

1 small onion, chopped

1½ pounds chicken breasts, cut into ½-inch cubes

¼ cup fresh lemon juice

1 teaspoon dried cilantro

1 tablespoon ground cumin

Salt and ground black pepper, to taste

½ cup fresh cilantro, chopped

1 medium celery root, chopped

1 teaspoon dried basil

1 teaspoon dried basil

1 tablespoon red chili powder

1 cup chicken broth

- In the pot of Instant Pot Mini, place all the ingredients except fresh cilantro and stir to combine.
- Secure the lid and turn to "Seal" position.
- Cook on "Manual" with "High Pressure" for about 10 minutes.
- Press the "Cancel" and allow a "Natural" release.
- Carefully, remove the lid and mix in the cilantro.
- Serve hot.

Per Serving: Calories: 370; Total Fat: 13.8g; Saturated Fat: 3.8g; Protein: 51.6g; Carbs: 7.3g; Fiber: 2.3g; Sugar: 3g

Chicken & Corn Chili

Serves: 4 / Preparation time: 15 minutes / Cooking time: 18 minutes

2 tablespoons olive oil

2 teaspoons garlic, minced

2 cups tomatoes, chopped finely

1 teaspoon dried oregano, crushed

1 teaspoon ground cumin

10 ounces fresh corn kernel

¾ cup cooked bacon, chopped and divided

1 cup onion, chopped

2 cups cooked chicken, chopped

¼ cup jalapeño peppers, chopped

2 teaspoons red chili powder

2 cups chicken broth

5 ounces cream cheese, softened

¼ cup Pepper Jack cheese, shredded

- Add the oil in an Instant Pot Mini and select "Sauté". Now, add the onion and cook for about 5 minutes.
- Press the "Cancel" and stir in the remaining ingredients except cream cheese, bacon and Pepper Jack cheese.
- Secure the lid and turn to "Seal" position.
- Select "Soup" and just use the default time of 10 minutes.
- Press the "Cancel" and allow a "Quick" release.
- Carefully, remove the lid and mix in the cream cheese and ½ cup of the bacon.
- Select "Sauté" and cook for about 3 minutes.
- Press the "Cancel" and serve hot with the topping of remaining bacon and Pepper Jack cheese.

Per Serving: Calories: 838; Total Fat: 39.5g; Saturated Fat: 14.3g; Protein: 49.9g; Carbs: 82.5g; Fiber: 13.1g; Sugar: 16.8g

Chicken & Tomato Curry

Serves: 4 / Preparation time: 15 minutes / Cooking time: 21 minutes

1 tablespoon coconut oil

1¼ pounds skinless, boneless chicken breasts, cubed

2 tablespoons curry powder

½ cup onion, sliced thinly

1 tablespoon fresh ginger, minced

1 tablespoon garlic, minced

2 cups tomatoes, chopped

1 (8-ounce) can tomato sauce

1 (14-ounce) can light coconut milk

Salt and ground black pepper, to taste

¼ cup fresh cilantro, chopped

- Add the butter in the Instant Pot Mini and select "Sauté". Now, add the chicken pieces and cook for about 4-5 minutes.
- With a slotted spoon, transfer the chicken breasts into a bowl.
- Add curry powder and cook for about 30 seconds.
- Add the onion, ginger and garlic and cook for about 30 seconds.
- Press the "Cancel" and stir in the tomatoes, tomato sauce, coconut milk, salt and black pepper.
- Secure the lid and turn to "Seal" position.
- Cook on "Manual" with "High Pressure" for about 12 minutes.
- Press the "Cancel" and allow a "Quick" release.
- Carefully, remove the lid and mix in the cooked chicken.
- Secure the lid and turn to "Seal" position.
- Cook on "Manual" with "High Pressure" for about 3 minutes.
- Press the "Cancel" and allow a "Natural" release.
- Carefully, remove the lid and serve hot with the garnishing of cilantro.

Per Serving: Calories: 701; Total Fat: 39g; Saturated Fat: 28.2g; Protein: 74.3g; Carbs: 16.9g; Fiber: 5.7g; Sugar: 8.9g

Chicken & Veggie Curry

Serves: 4 / Preparation time: 20 minutes / Cooking time: 11 minutes

14 ounces coconut milk, divided

3 tablespoons red curry paste

1 pound boneless chicken breasts, cut into thin bite-size pieces

¼ cup chicken broth

1 cup carrots, peeled and sliced

1 cup red bell pepper, seeded and cubed

½ cup canned bamboo shoots, sliced

½ cup onion, cubed

4 Kaffir lime leaves, slightly bruised

2 teaspoons brown sugar

1¾ tablespoons fish sauce

1 tablespoon fresh lime juice

12 fresh Thai basil leaves

- Add half of the coconut milk and curry paste in the Instant Pot Mini and select "Sauté". Cook for about 1-2 minutes.
- Press the "Cancel" and stir in the remaining coconut milk, chicken and broth.
- Secure the lid and turn to "Seal" position.
- Cook on "Manual" with "High Pressure" for about 4 minutes.
- Press the "Cancel" and allow a "Quick" release.
- Carefully, remove the lid and mix in the remaining ingredients except basil.
- Select "Sauté" and cook for about 4-5 minutes.
- Press the "Cancel" and stir in the basil leaves.
- Serve hot.

Per Serving: Calories: 532; Total Fat: 35.7g; Saturated Fat: 24.4g; Protein: 37.1g; Carbs: 17g; Fiber: 4g; Sugar: 9.2g

Sweet & Sour Shredded Chicken

Serves: 2 / Preparation time: 15 minutes / Cooking time: 7 minutes

For Sauce

¼ cup rice vinegar

¼ cup honey

2 tablespoons soy sauce

1 tablespoon olive oil

½ of yellow onion, chopped roughly

1 tablespoon garlic, minced

1 teaspoon fresh ginger, minced

1 teaspoon red pepper flakes, crushed

Salt and freshly ground black pepper, required

For Chicken

2 (6-ounce) boneless, skinless chicken breasts, halved lengthwise

½ tablespoon cornstarch

1 tablespoon water

- For sauce: in a bowl, add all ingredients and beat until well combined.
- In the bottom of Instant Pot Mini, place the chicken breast halves and top with the sauce.
- Secure the lid and turn to "Seal" position.
- Cook on "Manual" with "High Pressure" for about 5 minutes.
- Press the "Cancel" and allow a "Quick" release.
- Carefully, remove the lid and with tongs, transfer the chicken breast halves into a bowl.
- With 2 forks, shred chicken.
- In a bowl, dissolve the cornstarch into water.
- Now, select "Sauté" and add cornstarch mixture, stirring continuously.
- Cook for about 2 minutes or until desired thickness, stirring occasionally.
- Add the shredded chicken and stir to combine.
- Press the "Cancel" and serve hot.

Per Serving: Calories: 571; Total Fat: 19.9g; Saturated Fat: 4.5g; Protein: 51.1g; Carbs: 43.1g; Fiber: 1.3g; Sugar: 36.4g

Creamy Shredded Chicken

Serves: 4 / Preparation time: 15 minutes / Cooking time: 18 minutes

4 (4-ounce) chicken breasts

1 package ranch dressing mix

1 cup mayonnaise

¼ cup scallion, chopped

½ cup chicken broth

8 ounces cream cheese, softened

2 cups cheddar cheese, shredded

- In the bottom of Instant Pot Mini, place the chicken breasts, cream cheese and broth and sprinkle with ranch dressing mix.
- Secure the lid and turn to "Seal" position.
- Cook on "Manual" with "High Pressure" for about 15 minutes.
- Press the "Cancel" and allow a "Natural" release for about 5 minutes and then allow a "Quick" release.
- Carefully, remove the lid and with tongs, transfer chicken breasts into a bowl.
- With 2 forks, shred the chicken breasts.
- Now, select "Sauté" and add the cream cheese, beating continuously.
- Add the shredded chicken and mayonnaise and stir to combine well.
- Press the "Cancel" and serve immediately with the topping of cheddar cheese and scallion.

Per Serving: Calories: 879; Total Fat: 66.7g; Saturated Fat: 29.6g; Protein: 52.5g; Carbs: 17.2g; Fiber: 0.2g; Sugar: 4.6g

Chicken with Pineapple

Serves: 4 / Preparation time: 15 minutes / Cooking time: 10 minutes

For Sauce

1/2 cup homemade tomato sauce

2 tbsp water

2 tbsp unsweetened coconut milk

1 tbsp apple cider vinegar

1 tbsp brown sugar

1/2 tsp ground mustard

1 tsp crushed red pepper flakes

1 cup whipping cream

Pinch of salt

Ground black pepper, as required

For Chicken

2 (3-ounce) skinless chicken drumsticks

1/2 cup fresh pineapple, cut into small pieces

1/2 tbsp freshly squeezed lime juice

- For sauce: in a large bowl, add all the ingredients and mix well.
- Add the chicken drumsticks and coat with the sauce complete.
- Place the pineapple pieces in the pot of Instant Pot evenly.
- Place the chicken drumsticks on top of the pineapple in a single layer.
- Pour sauce over drumsticks evenly.
- Secure the lid and turn to "Seal" position.
- Cook on "Manual" with "High Pressure" for about 10 minutes.
- Press the "Cancel" and allow a "Quick" release.
- Carefully, remove the lid and serve hot with a drizzling of the lime juice.

Per Serving: Calories: 407; Total Fat: 17.2g; Saturated Fat: 8.2g; Protein: 35.5g; Carbs: 13.9g; Fiber: 1.9g; Sugar: 10.9g

Chicken with Olives

Serves: 4 / Preparation time: 15 minutes / Cooking time: 25 minutes

1 tablespoon olive oil

½ pound tomatoes, crushed slightly

1 teaspoon dried oregano, crushed

Salt, to taste

1/3 cup green olives, pitted

4 bone-in chicken leg quarters

2 garlic cloves, crushed

¼ teaspoon red pepper flakes, crushed

1/3 cup chicken broth

1 tablespoon fresh basil leaves, torn

- Add the oil in an Instant Pot Mini and select "Sauté". Now, add the chicken leg quarters and cook for about 4-5 minutes.
- With a slotted spoon, transfer the chicken leg quarters onto a plate.
- In the pot, add the tomatoes with all juice, garlic, oregano, red pepper flakes and salt and cook for about 1 minute, scraping up the brown bits from the bottom.
- Press the "Cancel" and stir in the cooked chicken and broth.
- Secure the lid and turn to "Seal" position.
- Cook on "Manual" with "High Pressure" for about 14 minutes.
- Press the "Cancel" and allow a "Quick" release.
- Carefully, remove the lid and select "Sauté".
- Stir in the olives and basil and cook for about 5 minutes.
- Press the "Cancel" and serve hot.

Per Serving: Calories: 336; Total Fat: 24.7g; Saturated Fat: 6g; Protein: 30g; Carbs: 3.8g; Fiber: 1.3g; Sugar: 1.6g

Chicken with Salsa

Serves: 4 / Preparation time: 15 minutes / Cooking time: 20 minutes

4 (6-ounce) skinless, boneless frozen chicken breasts

1 cup tomato sauce

2 tablespoons fresh lime juice

1 cup mozzarella cheese, grated

1 cup mild salsa

Salt and ground black pepper, as required

- In the pot of Instant Pot Mini, place all the ingredients except cheese and stir to combine.
- Secure the lid and turn to "Seal" position.
- Cook on "Manual" with "High Pressure" for about 12 minutes.
- Press the "Cancel" and allow a "Quick" release.
- Meanwhile, preheat the oven to broiler. Grease a baking dish.
- Carefully, remove the lid and with tongs, transfer the chicken thighs onto the prepared baking dish.
- Now, select "Sauté" and cook for about 2-3 minutes, stirring continuously.
- Press the "Cancel" and spread the sauce over the chicken breasts evenly.
- Sprinkle the sauce with the cheese.
- Broil for about 4-5 minutes.
- Serve warm.

Per Serving: Calories: 264; Total Fat: 7.6g; Saturated Fat: 3.1g; Protein: 41.5g; Carbs: 6.5g; Fiber: 1.1g; Sugar: 4.4g

Herbed Chicken Breasts

Serves: 6 / Preparation time: 15 minutes / Cooking time: 13 minutes

4 (4-ounce) boneless, skinless chicken breasts

1 teaspoon garlic powder

1 tablespoon coconut oil

½ teaspoon dried basil, crushed

Salt and ground black pepper, to taste

½ teaspoon dried oregano, crushed

- Season the chicken breasts with garlic powder, salt and black pepper generously.
- Place the oil in the Instant Pot Mini and select "Sauté". Now, add the chicken breasts and herbs and cook for about 3-4 minute per side.
- Press the "Cancel" and with a slotted spoon, transfer chicken breasts onto a plate.
- Arrange a steamer trivet in the bottom of an Instant Pot Mini and pour 1½ cups of water.
- Place the chicken breasts on top of the trivet.
- Secure the lid and turn to "Seal" position.
- Cook on "Manual" with "High Pressure" for about 5 minutes.
- Press the "Cancel" and allow a "Quick" release.
- Carefully, remove the lid and transfer the chicken breasts onto a platter.
- Set aside for about 5 minutes before serving.

Per Serving: Calories: 248; Total Fat: 11.8g; Saturated Fat: 5.3g; Protein: 33g; Carbs: 0.6g; Fiber: 0.2g; Sugar: 0.2g

Spicy Chicken Thighs

Serves: 4 / Preparation time: 15 minutes / Cooking time: 29 minutes

¾ cup yogurt

2 tablespoons fresh lemon juice

1 tablespoon fresh ginger, chopped roughly

1 green chili pepper, chopped roughly

1 tablespoon paprika

1 teaspoon ground cumin

1 teaspoon ground turmeric

6 bone-in, skinless chicken thighs

¼ cup chicken broth

½ cup onion, chopped roughly

1 tablespoon garlic, chopped roughly

1 tablespoon brown sugar

1 tablespoon ground coriander

1 teaspoon garam masala

Salt and ground black pepper, to taste

- In a blender, add all ingredients except chicken thighs and pulse until smooth.
- In the pot of Instant Pot Mini, add chicken thighs and yogurt mixture and stir to combine.
- Secure the lid and turn to "Seal" position.
- Cook on "Manual" with "High Pressure" for about 15 minutes.
- Press the "Cancel" and allow a "Quick" release.
- Meanwhile, preheat the oven to broiler. Line a broiler pan with a greased parchment paper.
- Carefully, remove the lid and with tongs, transfer the chicken thighs onto a plate.
- Now, select "Sauté" and cook for about 8-10 minutes or until sauce becomes thick, stirring occasionally.
- Press the "Cancel" and transfer the sauce into a bowl.
- Coat the chicken thighs with sauce evenly and arrange onto the prepared broiler pan.
- Broil chicken thighs for about 2 minutes per side.

Per Serving: Calories: 553; Total Fat: 20.1g; Saturated Fat: 5.9g; Protein: 77.6g; Carbs: 10.3g; Fiber: 1.4g; Sugar: 6.6g

Sweet & Sour Chicken Thighs

Serves: 4 / Preparation time: 15 minutes / Cooking time: 22 minutes

1 tablespoon olive oil

¾ teaspoon fresh ginger, minced

4 (4-ounce) skinless, boneless chicken thighs

½ cup tomato sauce

2 tablespoons maple syrup

1 tablespoons cornstarch

2 tablespoons fresh parsley, chopped

2 garlic cloves, minced

Salt and ground black pepper, to taste

¼ cup tamari

2 tablespoons fresh lemon juice

1 tablespoons water

- Add the oil in an Instant Pot Mini and select "Sauté". Now, add the garlic and cook for about 1 minute.
- Add the chicken thighs, salt and black pepper and cook for about 5 minutes or until browned from completely.
- Press the "Cancel" and stir in the tomato sauce, tamari, maple syrup and lemon juice.
- Secure the lid and turn to "Seal" position.
- Cook on "Manual" with "High Pressure" for about 10 minutes.
- Press the "Cancel" and allow a "Quick" release.
- Meanwhile, in a small bowl, add the cornstarch and water and mix well.
- Carefully, remove the lid and select "Sauté".
- Add the cornstarch mixture, stirring continuously.
- Cook for about 4-5 minutes, stirring continuously.
- Press the "Cancel" and serve hot with the garnishing of parsley.

Per Serving: Calories: 230; Total Fat: 7.8g; Saturated Fat: 2.1g; Protein: 27.9g; Carbs: 12.3g; Fiber: 0.8g; Sugar: 7.8g

Roasted Whole Chicken

Serves: 4 / Preparation time: 15 minutes / Cooking time: 31 minutes

1 (2½-pound) whole chicken, neck and giblet removed

1 tablespoon cayenne pepper

2 tablespoon olive oil

Salt and ground black pepper, to taste

1½ cups chicken broth

- Sprinkle the chicken with cayenne pepper, salt and black pepper generously.
- Add the oil in an Instant Pot Mini and select "Sauté". Now, add the chicken and cook for about 5-6 minute or until browned.
- Transfer the chicken onto a plate.
- Arrange a steamer trivet in the bottom of an Instant Pot Mini and pour the broth.
- Arrange the chicken on top of the trivet, breast side up.
- Secure the lid and turn to "Seal" position.
- Cook on "Manual" with "High Pressure" for about 20-25 minutes.
- Press the "Cancel" and allow a "Quick" release.
- Carefully, remove the lid and place the chicken onto a cutting board.
- Cut into desired sized pieces and serve.

Per Serving: Calories: 617; Total Fat: 28.8g; Saturated Fat: 7g; Protein: 84g; Carbs: 1.1g; Fiber: 0g; Sugar: 0g

Turkey with Quinoa & Chickpeas

Serves: 4 / Preparation time: 15 minutes / Cooking time: 20 minutes

1½ tablespoons olive oil

6 ounces skinless, boneless turkey breast, cubed

1 medium onion, chopped	1 small sweet potato, peeled and chopped
2 garlic cloves, minced	1 tablespoon red chili powder
¼ teaspoon red pepper flakes, crushed	¼ teaspoon ground cumin
¼ teaspoon ground coriander	Salt, to taste
1 cup canned chickpeas, rinsed and drained	¼ cup uncooked quinoa
1 cup tomatoes, chopped finely	1½ cups chicken broth
1 tablespoon fresh lemon juice	2 tablespoons fresh cilantro, chopped

- Add the oil in an Instant Pot Mini and select "Sauté". Now, add the turkey and cook for about 5 minutes or until browned completely.
- With a slotted spoon, transfer the turkey into a bowl.
- In the pot, add the onion and cook for about 5 minutes.
- Add the sweet potato and cook for about 5 minutes.
- Add the garlic and spices and cook for about 1 minute.
- Press the "Cancel" and stir in the turkey, chickpeas, quinoa, tomato and broth.
- Secure the lid and turn to "Seal" position.
- Cook on "Manual" with "High Pressure" for about 4 minutes.
- Press the "Cancel" and allow a "Natural" release for about 6 minutes and then allow a "Quick" release.
- Carefully, remove the lid and mix in the lemon juice and cilantro.
- Serve hot.

Per Serving: Calories: 376; Total Fat: 11.5g; Saturated Fat: 1.9g; Protein: 13.9.g; Carbs: 46.7g; Fiber: 11.8g; Sugar: 9.2g

Turkey Stuffed Bell Peppers

Serves: 4 / Preparation time: 25 minutes / Cooking time: 18 minutes

For Sauce

2 tablespoons chipotle in adobo sauce, minced

½ cup sour cream

2 teaspoons fresh lime juice

1 teaspoon fresh lime zest, grated

1/8 teaspoon garlic powder

For Bell Peppers

1 pound ground turkey

2 scallions, chopped

1 jalapeño pepper, chopped

2 teaspoons red chili powder

1 teaspoon garlic powder

4 bell peppers, tops and seeds removed

1 cup water

5 ounces chopped canned green chilies

½ cup Panko breadcrumbs

1 teaspoon ground cumin

Salt, to taste

4 Pepper Jack cheese slices

- For sauce: in a bowl, add all the ingredients and mix until well combined.
- Refrigerate, covered until serving.
- In a large bowl, add the turkey, scallions, green chilies, jalapeño pepper, breadcrumbs and spices and mix until well combined.
- Stuff each bell pepper with the turkey mixture evenly.
- Arrange a steamer basket in the bottom of an Instant Pot Mini and pour 1 cup of water.
- Arrange the stuffed bell peppers in the steamer basket.
- Secure the lid and turn to "Seal" position.
- Cook on "Manual" with "High Pressure" for about 15 minutes.
- Press the "Cancel" and allow a "Natural" release for about 10 minutes and then allow a "Quick" release.
- Meanwhile, preheat the oven to broiler.
- Carefully, remove the lid and transfer the bell peppers onto a broiler pan.
- Place 1 cheese slice over each bell pepper and broil for about 2-3 minutes or until cheese is melted.
- Remove from oven and transfer the bell peppers onto serving plates.
- Top each bell pepper with the sauce and serve.

Per Serving: Calories: 613; Total Fat: 31.1g; Saturated Fat: 12.4g; Protein: 46.3g; Carbs: 47g; Fiber: 13.3g; Sugar: 22.1g

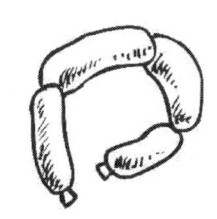

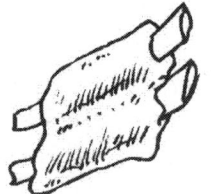

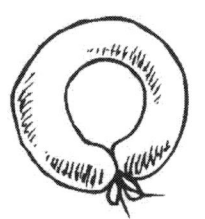

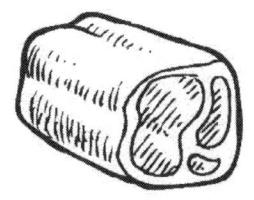

PORK RECIPES

Contents

Pork & Bok Choy Soup	42
Ground Pork & Green Beans Soup	43
Ground Pork & Cabbage Soup	44
Pork & Veggie Stew	45
Ham & Split Peas Soup	46
Pork & Corn Stew	47
Pork Sausage & Veggie Stew	48
Pork Vindaloo	49
Pork Curry	50
Pork Ribs in Mustard Sauce	51
Pork with Pineapple	52
Pork with Mushrooms	53
Creamy Pork Chops	54
Pork Chops with Apple	55
BBQ Pork Spare Ribs	56
BBQ Pork Baby Back Ribs	57
Pork Tenderloin with Fruit	58
Spicy Pork Butt	59
Beer Braised Pulled Pork	60
Lemony Pulled Pork	61
Pork Sausage with Quinoa	62
Pork Sausage with Potato Mash	63

Pork & Bok Choy Soup

Serves: 4 / Preparation time: 15 minutes / Cooking time: 23 minutes

2 tablespoons peanut oil

6 garlic cloves, minced

1 pound pork shoulder, cut into chunks

2 tablespoons soy sauce

2 tablespoons Chinese fermented broad bean paste

2 teaspoons sugar

Salt, to taste

3 cups bok choy, chopped

½ onion, sliced

1 teaspoon fresh ginger, minced

2 tablespoons black vinegar

2 teaspoons Szechuan peppers, crushed

3 cups water

¼ cup fresh cilantro, chopped

- Add the oil in an Instant Pot Mini and select "Sauté". Now, add the onion, garlic and ginger and cook for about 2-3 minutes.
- Press the "Cancel" and stir in the remaining ingredients except bok choy and cilantro.
- Secure the lid and turn to "Seal" position.
- Cook on "Manual" with "High Pressure" for about 20 minutes.
- Press the "Cancel" and allow a "Natural" release for about 10 minutes and then allow a "Quick" release.
- Carefully, remove the lid and mix in the bok choy.
- Immediately, secure the lid and turn to "Seal" position for about 10 minutes.
- Serve immediately with the garnishing of cilantro.

Per Serving: Calories: 440; Total Fat: 31.7g; Saturated Fat: 10.1g; Protein: 8.5g; Carbs: 8.5g; Fiber: 1.6g; Sugar: 4g

Ground Pork & Green Beans Soup

Serves: 4 / Preparation time: 15 minutes / Cooking time: 38 minutes

1 tablespoon olive oil

1 pound lean ground pork

1 onion, chopped

1 tablespoon garlic, minced

2 teaspoons dried thyme, crushed

1 teaspoon ground cumin

3 cups fresh tomatoes, chopped finely

¾ pound fresh green beans, trimmed and cut into 1-inch pieces

3¼ cups beef broth

Salt and ground black pepper, to taste

¼ cup Parmesan cheese, grated freshly

- Add the oil in an Instant Pot Mini and select "Sauté". Now, add the pork and cook for about 5 minutes or until browned completely.
- Add the onion, garlic, thyme, cumin and cook for about 3 minutes.
- Press the "Cancel" and stir in the tomatoes, green beans and broth.
- Secure the lid and turn to "Seal" position.
- Cook on "Manual" with "Low Pressure" for about 30 minutes.
- Press the "Cancel" and allow a "Quick" release.
- Carefully, remove the lid and mix in the salt and black pepper.
- Serve immediately with the garnishing of the Parmesan cheese.

Per Serving: Calories: 380; Total Fat: 23.6g; Saturated Fat: 1.8g; Protein: 28.4g; Carbs: 16g; Fiber: 5.4g; Sugar: 6.5g

Ground Pork & Cabbage Soup

Serves: 4 / Preparation time: 15 minutes / Cooking time: 30 minutes

1 tablespoon olive oil

1 small onion, chopped

½ head cabbage, chopped

¼ cup low-sodium soy sauce

Salt and ground black pepper, to taste

1 pound lean ground pork

1 cup carrot, peeled and shredded

3½ cups chicken broth

1 teaspoon ground ginger

- Add the oil in an Instant Pot Mini and select "Sauté". Now, add the pork and cook for about 5 minutes or until browned completely.
- Press the "Cancel" and stir in the remaining ingredients.
- Secure the lid and turn to "Seal" position.
- Cook on "Manual" with "High Pressure" for about 25 minutes.
- Press the "Cancel" and allow a "Quick" release.
- Carefully, remove the lid and serve immediately.

Per Serving: Calories: 341; Total Fat: 21.9g; Saturated Fat: 0.9g; Protein: 26.1g; Carbs: 11.6g; Fiber: 3.4g; Sugar: 6.6g

Pork & Veggie Stew

Serves: 4 / Preparation time: 20 minutes / Cooking time: 25 minutes

3 tablespoons olive oil, divided

Salt and ground black pepper, as required

1 onion, chopped

1 rutabaga, peeled and cubed

2 carrots, peeled and cut into big chunks

½ cup chicken broth

1¼ pounds pork shoulder, cubed

1 red bell pepper, seeded and chopped

2 garlic cloves, chopped

8 baby potatoes

1 (14-ounce) can diced tomatoes

- Add 2 tablespoons of the oil in the Instant Pot Mini and select "Sauté". Now, add the pork, salt and black pepper and cook for about 4-5 minutes.
- With a slotted spoon, transfer the pork onto a plate.
- In the pot, add the remaining oil, bell pepper, onions and cook for about 3 minutes.
- Press the "Cancel" and stir in the cooked pork and remaining ingredients.
- Secure the lid and turn to "Seal" position.
- Cook on "Manual" with "High Pressure" for about 20 minutes.
- Press the "Cancel" and allow a "Quick" release.
- Carefully, remove the lid and serve hot.

Per Serving: Calories: 548; Total Fat: 35.5g; Saturated Fat: 10.5g; Protein: 30.8g; Carbs: 28g; Fiber: 6.6g; Sugar: 12.9g

Ham & Split Peas Soup

Serves: 4 / Preparation time: 20 minutes / Cooking time: 23 minutes

2 tablespoon olive oil

1 small onion, diced

2 celery stalks, chopped

4 cups vegetable broth

Salt and ground black pepper, to taste

1 cup ham, cut into bite-sized pieces

1 large carrot, peeled and chopped

1¼ cups dry split peas

1 teaspoon garlic powder

- Add the oil in an Instant Pot Mini and select "Sauté". Now, add the ham and onion and cook for about 5 minutes.
- Press the "Cancel" and stir in the remaining ingredients.
- Secure the lid and turn to "Seal" position.
- Cook on "Manual" with "High Pressure" for about 18 minutes.
- Press the "Cancel" and allow a "Quick" release.
- Carefully, remove the lid and stir well.
- Serve hot.

Per Serving: Calories: 381; Total Fat: 12g; Saturated Fat: 2.5g; Protein: 26.1g; Carbs: 43.5g; Fiber: 17.2g; Sugar: 7.5g

Pork & Corn Stew

Serves: 4 / Preparation time: 15 minutes / Cooking time: 51 minutes

1 tablespoon olive oil

¾ pound boneless pork shoulder, trimmed and cubed

Salt and ground black Pepper, as required

2 garlic cloves, minced

1 teaspoon ground cumin

2 cups chicken broth

1 tablespoons cornstarch

1 small onion, chopped

1 tablespoon red chili powder

1 teaspoon ground coriander

1 tablespoon cold water

2 cups frozen corns, thawed

- Add the oil in an Instant Pot Mini and select "Sauté". Now, add the pork, salt and black pepper and cook for about 5 minutes or until browned completely.
- With a slotted spoon, transfer the pork into a bowl.
- In the pot, add the onion and cook for about 5 minutes.
- Add the garlic and spices and cook for about 1 minute.
- Press the "Cancel" and stir in the cooked pork and broth.
- Secure the lid and turn to "Seal" position.
- Cook on "Manual" with "High Pressure" for about 30 minutes.
- Press the "Cancel" and allow a "Natural" release for about 5 minutes and then allow a "Quick" release.
- Carefully, remove the lid and transfer the pork into a bowl.
- With 2 forks, shred the pork.
- In a small bowl, add the water and cornstarch and mix well.
- Now, select "Sauté" and add the cornstarch mixture, stirring continuously.
- Stir in the shredded pork and corn and cook for about 4-5 minutes.
- Press the "Cancel" and serve hot.

Per Serving: Calories: 258; Total Fat: 8.1g; Saturated Fat: 1.9g; Protein: 27.3g; Carbs: 20.6g; Fiber: 2.9g; Sugar: 3.7g

Pork Sausage & Veggie Stew

Serves: 4 / Preparation time: 20 minutes / Cooking time: 24 minutes

1 tablespoon coconut oil

1 pound andouille pork sausage

2 bell peppers, seeded and chopped

2 celery stalks, chopped

2 carrots, peeled and chopped

1 medium onion, sliced

6 garlic cloves, minced

3 cups tomatoes, chopped

2 cups chicken broth

¼ cup fresh parsley, minced

1 teaspoon dried thyme

1 bay leaf

½ teaspoon red pepper flakes, crushed

½ teaspoon smoked paprika

¼ teaspoon cayenne pepper

Sea salt and ground black pepper, as required

2 drops hot sauce

- Add the oil in an Instant Pot Mini and select "Sauté". Now, add the sausage and cook for about 8-10 minutes.
- With a slotted spoon, transfer the sausage and onto a plate.
- In the pot, add the bell peppers, celery, carrots and onion and cook for about 2-3 minutes.
- Add the garlic and cook for about 1 minute.
- Add the tomatoes and broth and bring to a boil.
- Meanwhile, cut the sausage into bite-sized pieces.
- Press the "Cancel" and stir in the sausage and remaining ingredients except the hot sauce.
- Secure the lid and turn to "Seal" position.
- Select the "Soup" and just use the default time of 10 minutes.
- Press the "Cancel" and allow a "Quick" release.
- Carefully, remove the lid and mix in the hot sauce.
- Serve hot.

Per Serving: Calories: 328; Total Fat: 15.7g; Saturated Fat: 6.7g; Protein: 27.4g; Carbs: 20.2g; Fiber: 5.4g; Sugar: 9.8g

Pork Vindaloo

Serves: 4 / Preparation time: 20 minutes / Cooking time: 26 minutes

4 whole red chilies, stemmed

2 teaspoons cumin seeds

½ teaspoon mustard seeds

1 (2-inch) piece cinnamon stick

1 teaspoon black peppercorns

4 whole cloves

1 teaspoon ground turmeric

Salt, to taste

1 tablespoon fresh ginger, minced

1 tablespoon garlic, minced

2 teaspoons tamarind paste

1 teaspoon brown sugar

¼ cup apple cider vinegar

1½ pounds boneless country style pork ribs, cut into 1½-inch pieces

3 tablespoons vegetable oil

2 cups onion, chopped finely

¾ cup water

- In a spice grinder, add the red chilies and all spices and grind into a fine powder.
- In a blender, add spice mixture, ginger, garlic, tamarind paste, brown sugar, vinegar and enough water and pulse until a smooth and thick paste is formed.
- Transfer the spice paste into a bowl with pork and mix well.
- Refrigerate to marinate overnight.
- Add 2 tablespoons of the oil in an Instant Pot Mini and select "Sauté". Now, add the onion and cook for about 5-6 minutes, stirring frequently.
- Add the remaining oil and pork and cook for about 4-5 minutes.
- Press the "Cancel" and stir in the water.
- Secure the lid and turn to "Seal" position.
- Cook on "Manual" with "High Pressure" for about 15 minutes.
- Press the "Cancel" and allow a "Natural" release.
- Carefully, remove the lid and serve hot.

Per Serving: Calories: 384; Total Fat: 16.8g; Saturated Fat: 4.1g; Protein: 45.9g; Carbs: 10.4g; Fiber: 2.2g; Sugar: 4.3g

Pork Curry

Serves: 4 / Preparation time: 15 minutes / Cooking time: 42 minutes

2 tablespoons olive oil

1½ pounds boneless pork butt roast, trimmed and cubed

Salt and ground black pepper, as required

2 onions, chopped finely

4 garlic cloves, minced

1 teaspoon ground cumin

1 teaspoon paprika

¼ teaspoon cayenne pepper

1 teaspoon mustard seeds

2 tablespoons all-purpose flour

1 (14½-ounce) can diced tomatoes

1 cup chicken broth

2 tablespoons red wine vinegar

1 teaspoon sugar

2 tablespoons fresh cilantro, chopped

- Add the oil in an Instant Pot Mini and select "Sauté". Now, add the pork, salt and black pepper and cook for about 4-5 minutes or until browned.
- With a slotted spoon, transfer the pork into a bowl.
- In the pot, add the onion and cook for about 4-5 minutes.
- Add the garlic and spices and cook for about 1 minute.
- Stir in flour and cook for about 1 minute.
- Press the "Cancel" and stir in the cooked pork and remaining ingredients except the cilantro.
- Secure the lid and turn to "Seal" position.
- Cook on "Manual" with "High Pressure" for about 30 minutes.
- Press the "Cancel" and allow a "Natural" release.
- Carefully, remove the lid and mix in the salt and black pepper.
- Serve hot with the garnishing of cilantro.

Per Serving: Calories: 507; Total Fat: 35.5g; Saturated Fat: 11.8g; Protein: 32.6g; Carbs: 15.3g; Fiber: 3g; Sugar: 6.4g

Pork Ribs in Mustard Sauce

Serves: 4 / Preparation time: 15 minutes / Cooking time: 34 minutes

½ tablespoon olive oil

Salt and ground black pepper, as required

2 garlic cloves, minced

1 tablespoon white vinegar

1 tablespoons soy sauce

¼ teaspoon dry mustard

½ tablespoon cold water

1 pound boneless pork ribs

1 small onion, chopped

¼ teaspoon fresh ginger, minced

2 tablespoons fresh pineapple juice

2 tablespoons brown sugar

½ tablespoon cornstarch

2 scallions, chopped

- Add the oil in an Instant Pot Mini and select "Sauté". Now, add the ribs, salt and black pepper and cook for about 5 minutes or until browned completely.
- With a slotted spoon, transfer the ribs into a bowl.
- In the pot, add the onion and cook for about 4-5 minutes.
- Add the garlic and ginger and cook for about 1 minute.
- Press the "Cancel" and stir in the cooked ribs, vinegar, pineapple juice, brown sugar and mustard.
- Secure the lid and turn to "Seal" position.
- Cook on "Manual" with "High Pressure" for about 20 minutes.
- Press the "Cancel" and allow a "Quick" release.
- Meanwhile in a small bowl, mix together corn starch and cold water.
- Carefully, remove the lid and with tongs, transfer the ribs into a bowl.
- Now, select Sauté and add the cornstarch mixture, stirring continuously.
- Cook for about 2-3 minutes or until desired thickness.
- Press the "Cancel" and stir in the ribs.
- Immediately, secure the lid and turn to "Seal" position for about 10 minutes.
- Serve hot with the garnishing of scallion.

Per Serving: Calories: 219; Total Fat: 5.8g; Saturated Fat: 1.6g; Protein: 30.5g; Carbs: 9.7g; Fiber: 0.7g; Sugar: 6.2g

Pork with Pineapple

Serves: 4 / Preparation time: 15 minutes / Cooking time: 20 minutes

15 ounces canned pineapple chunks in juice

1 tablespoon fresh ginger, grated

2 tablespoons brown sugar

2 tablespoons water

2 tablespoons olive oil, divided

1 onion, chopped

1 teaspoon dried oregano

3 garlic cloves, minced

2 tablespoons honey

1½ tablespoons soy sauce

1 tablespoon cornstarch

1 red bell pepper, seeded and chopped

1¼ pounds boneless pork stew meat

Salt and ground black pepper, to taste

- Drain the pineapple chunks, reserving the juice into a bowl.
- For sauce: in the bowl of pineapple juice, add the garlic, ginger, honey, brown sugar, soy sauce, water and cornstarch and beat until well combined.
- Add 1 tablespoon of the oil in the Instant Pot Mini and select "Sauté". Now, add the bell pepper and onion and cook for about 4-5 minutes.
- With a slotted spoon, transfer the onion mixture into a bowl.
- In the pot, place the remaining oil and cook the pork for about 4-5 minutes.
- Add the pineapple chunks, oregano, salt and black pepper and stir to combine.
- Press the "Cancel" and stir in the sauce.
- Secure the lid and turn to "Seal" position.
- Cook on "Manual" with "High Pressure" for about 10 minutes.
- Press the "Cancel" and allow a "Natural" release for about 5 minutes and then allow a "Quick" release.
- Carefully, remove the lid and mix in the cooked onion mixture.
- Serve hot.

Per Serving: Calories: 405; Total Fat: 12.4g; Saturated Fat: 2.8g; Protein: 36.1g; Carbs: 2.9g; Fiber: 2.9g; Sugar: 26.3g

Pork with Mushrooms

Serves: 4 / Preparation time: 15 minutes / Cooking time: 21 minutes

1 tablespoon olive oil

4 (6-ounce) bone-in pork chops

1 medium onion, chopped

1½ cups button mushrooms, chopped roughly

1 cup tomato sauce

2 garlic cloves, minced

Salt and ground black pepper, to taste

½ cup water

- Add the oil in an Instant Pot Mini and select "Sauté". Now, add the garlic and cook for about 1 minute.
- Add the pork chops, salt and black pepper and cook for about 5 minutes or until browned completely.
- Press the "Cancel" and stir in the mushrooms, tomato sauce and water.
- Secure the lid and turn to "Seal" position.
- Cook on "Manual" with "High Pressure" for about 15 minutes.
- Press the "Cancel" and allow a "Quick" release.
- Carefully, remove the lid and serve hot

Per Serving: Calories: 608; Total Fat: 40.6g; Saturated Fat: 16.4g; Protein: 40.2g; Carbs: 7.2g; Fiber: 1.8g; Sugar: 4.2g

Creamy Pork Chops

Serves: 4 / Preparation time: 15 minutes / Cooking time: 21 minutes

4 boneless pork chops

1 cup water

1 cup chicken broth

10 ounces canned cream of mushroom soup

1 cup sour cream

Salt and ground black pepper, to taste

2 teaspoons olive oil

2 tablespoons fresh parsley, chopped

- Rub the pork chops with salt and black pepper evenly.
- Add the oil in an Instant Pot Mini and select "Sauté". Now, add the pork chops and cook for about 3-4 minutes per side.
- With a slotted spoon, transfer the pork chops onto a plate.
- In the pot, add the broth and stir to combine, scraping the brown bits.
- Press the "Cancel" and stir in the cooked pork chops.
- Secure the lid and turn to "Seal" position.
- Cook on "Manual" with "High Pressure" for about 9 minutes.
- Press the "Cancel" and allow a "Natural" release.
- Carefully, remove the lid and with tongs, transfer the pork chops onto a platter.
- With a piece of the foil, cover the chops to keep warm.
- Now, select Sauté and stir in the mushroom soup.
- Cook for about 2 minutes.
- Press the "Cancel" and stir in the sour cream until well combined.
- Pour cream mixture over pork chops and serve.

Per Serving: Calories: 403; Total Fat: 29.8g; Saturated Fat: 13.8g; Protein: 28.7g; Carbs: 6.1g; Fiber: 0.1g; Sugar: 0.8g

Pork Chops with Apple

Serves: 4 / Preparation time: 15 minutes / Cooking time: 14 minutes

4 tablespoons butter

4 tablespoons brown sugar

1 teaspoon ground nutmeg

Salt and ground black pepper, to taste

2 apples, cored and sliced

1 tablespoon ground cinnamon

4 (5-ounce) pork chops

- In a large bowl, add the apples, brown sugar, cinnamon and nutmeg and toss to coat well.
- Add the butter in the Instant Pot Mini and select "Sauté". Now, add the apple mixture and cook for about 4 minutes, stirring occasionally.
- Meanwhile, season the pork chops with the salt and black pepper evenly.
- Press the "Cancel" and arrange the pork chops over the apples.
- Secure the lid and turn to "Seal" position.
- Select "Meat/Stew" and just use the default time of 10 minutes.
- Press the "Cancel" and allow a "Quick" release.
- Carefully, remove the lid and serve hot.

Per Serving: Calories: 655; Total Fat: 47.2g; Saturated Fat: 20.6g; Protein: 32.4g; Carbs: 25.9g; Fiber: 3.7g; Sugar: 20.5g

BBQ Pork Spare Ribs

Serves: 4 / Preparation time: 15 minutes / Cooking time: 30 minutes

1 pork spare rib rack

1 small onion, chopped roughly

¼ cup water

½ teaspoon liquid smoke

Salt and ground black pepper, to taste

½ cup apple cider

1 teaspoon vanilla extract

½ cup BBQ sauce

- Season the rib racks with salt and black pepper evenly.
- In the pot of Instant Pot Mini, place the rib rack and remaining ingredients except the BBQ sauce.
- Secure the lid and turn to "Seal" position.
- Cook on "Manual" with "High Pressure" for about 20 minutes.
- Meanwhile, preheat the oven to 400 degrees F.
- Press the "Cancel" and allow a "Natural" release.
- Carefully, remove the lid and place the rib rack onto a baking sheet.
- Spread the BBQ sauce over the rib racks evenly.
- Bake for about 5 minutes per side.
- Remove from the oven and serve hot.

Per Serving: Calories: 952; Total Fat: 73g; Saturated Fat: 27.4g; Protein: 51.9g; Carbs: 16.7g; Fiber: 0.6g; Sugar: 12.4g

BBQ Pork Baby Back Ribs

Serves: 4 / Preparation time: 15 minutes / Cooking time: 30 minutes

1½ pounds pork baby back ribs

4 garlic cloves, minced

2 tablespoons Italian seasoning

4 cups water

2 bay leaves

1 teaspoon fresh ginger, minced

Salt and ground black pepper, to taste

½ cup BBQ sauce

- In the pot of Instant Pot Mini, place the pork ribs and top with the remaining ingredients except the BBQ sauce.
- Secure the lid and turn to "Seal" position.
- Cook on "Manual" with "High Pressure" for about 20 minutes.
- Press the "Cancel" and allow a "Natural" release.
- Carefully, remove the lid and transfer the pork ribs onto a cutting board for about 5 minutes.
- With a paper towel, pat dry the ribs completely.
- In a bowl, add the ribs and BBQ sauce and mix well.
- Refrigerate, covered for about 2-3 hours.
- Preheat the oven to broiler.
- Broil the ribs for about 5 minutes per side.
- Remove from the oven and serve hot.

Per Serving: Calories: 695; Total Fat: 52.9g; Saturated Fat: 20.8g; Protein: 38.8g; Carbs: 13.4g; Fiber: 0.3g; Sugar: 8.8g

Pork Tenderloin with Fruit

Serves: 4 / Preparation time: 15 minutes / Cooking time: 40 minutes

1 1/3 pounds boneless pork tenderloin

2/3 cup fresh cherries, pitted

1/3 cup onion, chopped

Salt and ground black pepper, to taste

2 cups apples, cored and chopped

1/3 cup celery stalk, chopped

½ cup fresh apple juice

- In the pot of Instant Pot Mini, place all the ingredients and stir to combine.
- Secure the lid and turn to "Seal" position.
- Select "Soup" and just use the default time of 40 minutes.
- Press the "Cancel" and allow a "Quick" release.
- Carefully, remove the lid and serve hot.

Per Serving: Calories: 248; Total Fat: 4.4g; Saturated Fat: 1.4g; Protein: 29g; Carbs: 23.5g; Fiber: 3.4g; Sugar: 17.9g

Spicy Pork Butt

Serves: 4 / Preparation time: 15 minutes / Cooking time: 41 minutes

1 teaspoon dried oregano

1 teaspoon paprika

1 teaspoon ground coriander

1½ pounds pork butt, cut into 3-inch pieces

2 tablespoons olive oil

1 bay leaf

4 garlic cloves, minced

2 teaspoons red chili powder

1 teaspoon ground cumin

Salt and ground black pepper, to taste

½ small onion, chopped

1 cinnamon stick

1/3 cup fresh orange juice

- In a large bowl, add the oregano, spices, salt and black pepper and mix well.
- Add the pork pieces and coat with the spice mixture generously.
- Add the oil in an Instant Pot Mini and select "Sauté". Now, add the pork pieces and cook for about 4-5 minutes.
- With a slotted spoon, transfer the pork pieces into a bowl.
- In the pot, add the onion, bay leaf, and cinnamon stick and cook for about 4-5 minutes.
- Add the garlic and cook for about 1 minute.
- Press the "Cancel" and stir in the cooked pork pieces and orange juice.
- Secure the lid and turn to "Seal" position.
- Cook on "Manual" with "High Pressure" for about 30 minutes.
- Press the "Cancel" and allow a "Natural" release for about 10 minutes and then allow a "Quick" release.
- Carefully, remove the lid and with a slotted spoon, skim off the extra fat from the top.
- Stir the mixture well and serve.

Per Serving: Calories: 414; Total Fat: 18.9g; Saturated Fat: 4.9g; Protein: 53.8g; Carbs: 5.4g; Fiber: 1.2g; Sugar: 2.3g

Beer Braised Pulled Pork

Serves: 4 / Preparation time: 15 minutes / Cooking time: 35 minutes

1½ pounds quarter pork roast

Freshly ground black pepper, to taste

¾ cup root beer

2 tablespoons tomato puree

¾ tablespoon honey

½ tablespoon fresh lemon juice

½ teaspoon garlic salt

1¼ cups onion, sliced

¼ cup ketchup

1 tablespoon all-purpose flour

1 tablespoon Worcestershire sauce

- Season the pork roast with garlic salt and black pepper evenly.
- In a bowl, add the remaining ingredients and mix until well combined.
- In the pot of Instant Pot Mini, place the roast and top with the beer mixture.
- Secure the lid and turn to "Seal" position.
- Select "Meat/Stew" and just use the default time of 35 minutes.
- Press the "Cancel" and allow a "Natural" release for about 5 minutes and then allow a "Quick" release.
- Carefully, remove the lid and with a slotted spoon, discard the onions.
- With two forks, shred the pork meat and mix with the pan sauce.
- Serve hot.

Per Serving: Calories: 435; Total Fat: 16.2g; Saturated Fat: 5.9g; Protein: 50g; Carbs: 17.1g; Fiber: 1.3g; Sugar: 11.1g

Lemony Pulled Pork

Serves: 4 / Preparation time: 15 minutes / Cooking time: 25 minutes

1 garlic clove, minced finely

1 tablespoon olive oil

1½ pounds boneless pork shoulder, trimmed and cubed

4 tablespoons water

1 teaspoon dried rosemary

Salt and ground black pepper, to taste

3 tablespoon fresh lemon juice

- Add the oil in an Instant Pot Mini and select "Sauté". Now, add the cumin seeds and cook for about 30 seconds.
- For pork: in a large bowl, add the garlic, rosemary, oil, salt and black pepper and mix well.
- Add the pork and coat with the garlic mixture generously. Set aside for about 15-20 minutes.
- In the pot of Instant Pot Mini, place the pork, water and lemon juice and stir to combine.
- Secure the lid and turn to "Seal" position.
- Cook on "Manual" with "High Pressure" for about 25 minutes.
- Press the "Cancel" and allow a "Natural" release.
- Carefully, remove the lid and with a slotted spoon, transfer pork into a large bowl.
- With 2 forks, shred the meat.
- Top with cooking liquid and serve.

Per Serving: Calories: 278; Total Fat: 9.6.g; Saturated Fat: 2.7g; Protein: 44.7g; Carbs: 0.7g; Fiber: 0.2g; Sugar: 0.3g

Pork Sausage with Quinoa

Serves: 4 / Preparation time: 20 minutes / Cooking time: 24 minutes

2 teaspoons olive oil

1 onion, chopped

1 teaspoon dried oregano

Salt and ground black pepper, as required

1 cup canned petite diced tomatoes

¾ pound cabbage, sliced thinly

¾ pound Italian pork sausage

3 garlic cloves, minced

1 teaspoon paprika

1 cup chicken broth

½ cup dry quinoa

2 tablespoons fresh parsley, minced

- Add the oil in an Instant Pot Mini and select "Sauté". Now, add the sausage and cook for about 5 minutes.
- Add the onion, garlic, oregano, paprika, salt and pepper and cook for about 3-4 minutes.
- Press the "Cancel" and stir in the broth and diced tomatoes.
- Secure the lid and turn to "Seal" position.
- Cook on "Manual" with "High Pressure" for about 12 minutes.
- Press the "Cancel" and allow a "Quick" release.
- Carefully, remove the lid and mix in the quinoa and then, place the cabbage on top.
- Secure the lid and turn to "Seal" position.
- Cook on "Manual" with "High Pressure" for about 3 minutes.
- Press the "Cancel" and allow a "Quick" release.
- Carefully, remove the lid and mix in the parsley.
- Serve hot.

Per Serving: Calories: 443; Total Fat: 28.4g; Saturated Fat: 8.4g; Protein: 22.9g; Carbs: 24.5g; Fiber: 5.2g; Sugar: 5.4g

Pork Sausage with Potato Mash

Serves: 3 / Preparation time: 20 minutes / Cooking time: 17 minutes

For Mash
4 floury potatoes, peeled and cubed into 1½-inch size
1 cup warm milk   ½ cup butter
2 teaspoons Dijon mustard   salt and ground black pepper, to taste
½ cup cheddar cheese, grated
For Sausage
6 thick pork sausages   2 teaspoons olive oil
½ cup onion jam   ½ cup red wine
½ cup water   1 tablespoon corn flour
1 tablespoon cold water   Salt and ground black pepper, to taste

- In the pot of Instant Pot Mini, place the potatoes and 1 cup of water.
- Secure the lid and turn to "Seal" position.
- Cook on "Manual" with "High Pressure" for about 4 minutes.
- Press the "Cancel" and allow a "Quick" release.
- Carefully, remove the lid and transfer the potatoes into a bowl.
- Cover the bowl and set aside.
- With a sharp knife, prick each sausage.
- Discard the cooking water from the pot of Instant Pot Mini and with paper towels pat dry it.
- Add the oil in an Instant Pot Mini and select "Sauté". Now, add the sausages and cook for about 2-3 minutes.
- Press the "Cancel" and stir in the onion jam, wine and water.
- Secure the lid and turn to "Seal" position.
- Cook on "Manual" with "High Pressure" for about 8 minutes.
- Meanwhile, with a fork, mash the potatoes well.
- Add the warm milk, butter, mustard, salt and black pepper and mix until smooth.
- Stir in the cheddar cheese and with a piece of foil, cover the bowl tightly to keep warm.
- In a small bowl, add the corn flour and cold water and mix until well combined.
- Press the "Cancel" and allow a "Quick" release.
- Carefully, remove the lid and select "Sauté".
- Add the corn flour mixture, stirring continuously.
- Cook for about 1-2 minutes, stirring continuously.
- Press the "Cancel" and serve hot alongside potato mash.

Per Serving: Calories: 726; Total Fat: 37.1g; Saturated Fat: 18.7g; Protein: 20.5g; Carbs: 74.4g; Fiber: 5.3g; Sugar: 29.6g

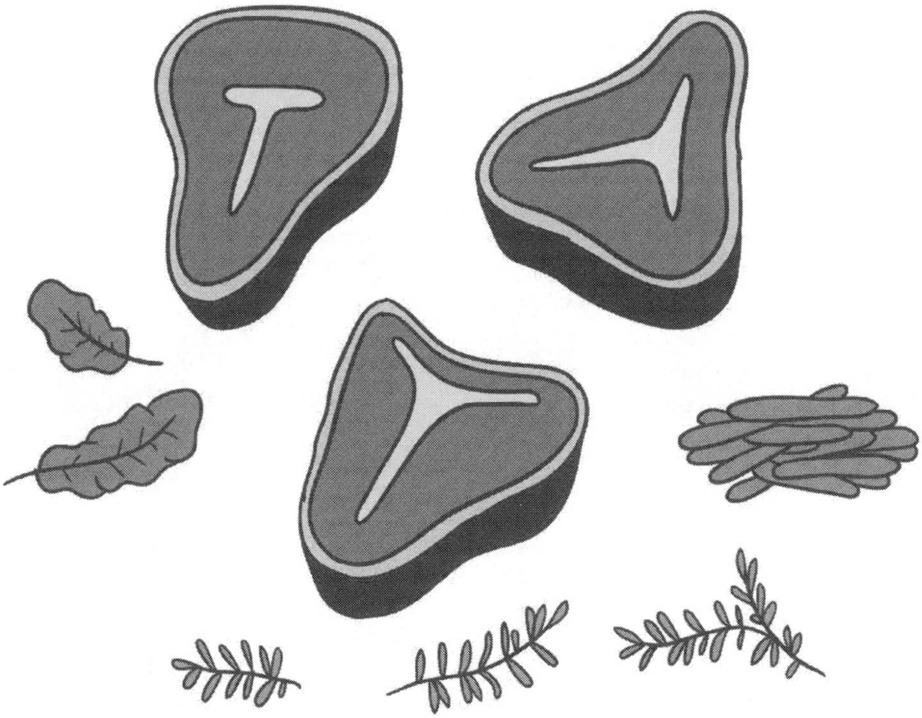

BEEF RECIPES

Contents

Beef & Mushroom Soup 66
Beef & Veggie Stew 67
Beef Meatballs Stew 68
Beef & Veggie Chili 69
Beef & Carrot Curry 70
Beef & Tomato Curry 71
Marinated Beef Curry 72
Beef & Chickpeas Curry 73
Beef with Green Beans 74
Beef with Broccoli 75
Beef with Bell Peppers 76
Honey Glazed Steak 77
Steak in Orange Sauce 78
Steak with Salsa 79
Beef with Tuna Sauce 80
Coffee Braised Pulled Beef 81
Ground Beef with Peas 82
Ground Beef with Cabbage & Rice 83
Ground Beef with Veggies & Oats 84
Beef Lasagna 85
Sweet & Sour Meatballs 86
Cheese Stuffed Beef Burgers 87

Beef & Mushroom Soup

Serves: 4 / Preparation time: 20 minutes / Cooking time: 28 minutes

2 teaspoons olive oil

2 medium carrots, peeled and chopped

1 large celery stalk, chopped

8 ounces fresh mushrooms, sliced

1½ cups water

1½ tablespoons fresh oregano, chopped

2 tablespoons garlic powder

1 pound sirloin steak, trimmed and cubed

1 bell pepper, seeded and chopped

1 onion, chopped

2 cups beef broth

1 cup tomatoes, crushed

1 bay leaf

Salt and ground black pepper, to taste

- Add the oil in an Instant Pot Mini and select "Sauté". Now, add the steak and cook for about 4-5 minutes or until browned.
- Add the carrots, bell pepper, celery, and onion and cook for about 2-3 minutes.
- Add the mushrooms and cook for about 4-5 minutes.
- Press the "Cancel" and stir in the remaining ingredients.
- Secure the lid and turn to "Seal" position.
- Now, select the "Soup" and just use the default time of 15 minutes.
- Press the "Cancel" and allow a "Quick" release.
- Carefully, remove the lid and serve hot.

Per Serving: Calories: 337; Total Fat: 11.1g; Saturated Fat: 3.4g; Protein: 41.3g; Carbs: 19.1g; Fiber: 6g; Sugar: 8g

Beef & Veggie Stew

Serves: 4 / Preparation time: 20 minutes / Cooking time: 31 minutes

¾ pound beef stew meat, trimmed and cubed

1 tablespoon olive oil

1 medium onion, cut into wedges

½ tablespoon Worcestershire sauce

2 potatoes, scrubbed and cubed

1 cup tomatoes, chopped finely

Salt and ground black pepper, as required

2 tablespoon all-purpose flour

2 garlic cloves, minced

½ teaspoon dried basil, crushed

1½ cups hot beef broth

2 medium carrots, peeled and cubed

2 celery stalks, chopped

2 tablespoons fresh cilantro, chopped

- In a large bowl, place the beef and flour and toss to coat well. Then, shake off the excess flour.
- Add the oil in an Instant Pot Mini and select "Sauté". Now, add the garlic and cook for about 1 minute.
- Add the beef and cook for about 5 minutes or until browned completely.
- Press the "Cancel" and stir in the onion, basil, Worcestershire sauce and broth and stir to combine.
- Secure the lid and turn to "Seal" position.
- Cook on "Manual" with "High Pressure" for about 20 minutes.
- Press the "Cancel" and allow a "Quick" release.
- Carefully, remove the lid and mix in the vegetables, salt and black pepper.
- Secure the lid and turn to "Seal" position.
- Cook on "Manual" with "High Pressure" for about 5 minutes.
- Press the "Cancel" and allow a "Natural" release for about 5 minutes and then allow a "Quick" release.
- Carefully, remove the lid and serve hot with the topping of cilantro.

Per Serving: Calories: 327; Total Fat: 9.6g; Saturated Fat: 2.7g; Protein: 30.9g; Carbs: 28.5g; Fiber: 4.7g; Sugar: 5.9g

Beef Meatballs Stew

Serves: 4 / Preparation time: 20 minutes / Cooking time: 10 minutes

For Meatballs

¾ pound ground beef

2 tablespoons fresh cilantro, minced

1 small egg, beaten

¼ teaspoon smoked paprika

3 tablespoons all-purpose flour

1 garlic clove, minced

1 white bread slice, soaked and squeezed

½ teaspoon Worcestershire sauce

Salt and ground black pepper, to taste

For Stew

1 tablespoon olive oil

1 potato, peeled and cubed

½ cup fresh peas, shelled

1½ cups chicken broth

1 cup carrot, peeled and cubed

1 tablespoon fresh lemon juice

- For meatballs: in a large bowl, add all the ingredients except the flour and mix until well combined.
- Make small equal sized balls from the mixture.
- Coat the balls with the flour evenly.
- Add the oil in an Instant Pot Mini and select "Sauté". Now, add the meatballs and cook for about 5 minutes or until browned completely.
- Press the "Cancel" and gently, stir in the remaining ingredients except the lemon juice.
- Secure the lid and turn to "Seal" position.
- Cook on "Manual" with "High Pressure" for about 5 minutes.
- Press the "Cancel" and allow a "Natural" release for about 5 minutes and then allow a "Quick" release.
- Carefully, remove the lid and serve hot with the drizzling of lemon juice.

Per Serving: Calories: 305; Total Fat: 10.5g; Saturated Fat: 3g; Protein: 31.7g; Carbs: 19.3g; Fiber: 2.9g; Sugar: 3.4g

Beef & Veggie Chili

Serves: 4 / Preparation time: 20 minutes / Cooking time: 40 minutes

1 tablespoon canola oil

½ green bell pepper, seeded and chopped

3 medium carrots, peeled and chopped

2 jalapeño peppers, chopped

1 tablespoon fresh parsley, chopped

3 teaspoons red chili powder

1 teaspoon ground cumin

16 ounces ground beef

1 small onion, chopped

2 large tomatoes, chopped finely

Salt and ground black pepper, to taste

1 tablespoon Worcestershire sauce

1 teaspoon paprika

- Add the oil in an Instant Pot Mini and select "Sauté". Now, add the beef and cook for about 4-5 minutes.
- Press the "Cancel" and stir in the remaining ingredients.
- Secure the lid and turn to "Seal" position.
- Select the "Stew/Meat" and just use the default time of 35 minutes.
- Press the "Cancel" and allow a "Natural" release.
- Carefully, remove the lid and serve hot.

Per Serving: Calories: 304; Total Fat: 11.4g; Saturated Fat: 3.3g; Protein: 36.5g; Carbs: 13.7g; Fiber: 4g; Sugar: 7.3g

Beef & Carrot Curry

Serves: 4 / Preparation time: 15 minutes / Cooking time: 33 minutes

2 tablespoons coconut oil
1¼ pounds beef stew meat, cut into 1-inch pieces
Salt and ground black pepper, as required
1 tablespoon fresh ginger, minced
1 jalapeño pepper, chopped finely
1 teaspoon red chili powder
1 tablespoon tomato sauce
1 cup onion, chopped
2 teaspoons garlic, minced
1 tablespoon curry powder
1 teaspoon ground cumin
2 cups beef broth
1½ cups carrots, peeled and cut into 1-inch pieces
2 cups unsweetened coconut milk
¼ cup fresh cilantro, chopped

- Add the oil in an Instant Pot Mini and select "Sauté". Now, add the beef, salt and black pepper and cook for about 4-5 minutes or until browned completely.
- With a slotted spoon, transfer the beef into a bowl.
- In the pot, add the onion, ginger, garlic and jalapeño pepper and cook for about 4-5 minutes.
- Press the "Cancel" and stir in the beef, spices and broth.
- Secure the lid and turn to "Seal" position.
- Cook on "Manual" with "High Pressure" for about 15 minutes.
- Press the "Cancel" and allow a "Quick" release.
- Carefully, remove the lid and mix in the carrots.
- Secure the lid and turn to "Seal" position.
- Cook on "Manual" with "High Pressure" for about 5 minutes.
- Press the "Cancel" and allow a "Natural" release for about 10 minutes and then allow a "Quick" release.
- Carefully, remove the lid and mix in the coconut milk.
- Now, select "Sauté" and cook for about 2-3 minutes.
- Press the "Cancel" and stir in the cilantro.
- Serve immediately.

Per Serving: Calories: 664; Total Fat: 45.5g; Saturated Fat: 34.9g; Protein: 49.5g; Carbs: 17.3g; Fiber: 5.5g; Sugar: 8.1g

Beef & Tomato Curry

Serves: 4 / Preparation time: 15 minutes / Cooking time: 30 minutes

2 large tomatoes, chopped roughly

4 garlic cloves, chopped roughly

1 teaspoon garam masala

½ teaspoons ground coriander

Salt and ground black pepper, to taste

1 small onion, chopped roughly

½ cup fresh cilantro, chopped

1 teaspoon ground cumin

½ teaspoon cayenne pepper

1½ pounds beef stew meat, cubed

- In a blender, add all the ingredients except the beef and pulse until smooth.
- In the pot of Instant Pot Mini, place the beef and top with the tomato mixture.
- Secure the lid and turn to "Seal" position.
- Cook on "Manual" with "High Pressure" for about 30 minutes.
- Press the "Cancel" and allow a "Quick" release.
- Carefully, remove the lid and serve hot.

Per Serving: Calories: 347; Total Fat: 11g; Saturated Fat: 4.1g; Protein: 53g; Carbs: 6.6g; Fiber: 53g; Sugar: 3.2g

Marinated Beef Curry

Serves: 4 / Preparation time: 15 minutes / Cooking time: 30 minutes

For Beef Marinade

½ cup coconut flakes

1 tablespoon ginger paste

2 tablespoons ground coriander

1 teaspoon garam masala

Salt and ground black pepper, as required

1 medium onion, chopped finely

1 tablespoon garlic paste

1 tablespoon red chili powder

½ teaspoon ground turmeric

1 pound boneless beef, cubed

For Curry

2 tablespoons coconut oil

1 onion, chopped

½ teaspoon garlic paste

4-6 curry leaves

½ teaspoon garam masala

¾ teaspoon mustard seed

½ teaspoon ginger paste

4 green chilies, chopped

1 teaspoon ground coriander

¼ teaspoon ground turmeric

- For marinade: in a large bowl, add all the ingredients except the beef and mix until well combined.
- Add the beef and coat with the mixture generously.
- Set aside at room temperature for about 30 minutes.
- In the pot of Instant Pot Mini, place the beef with marinade.
- Secure the lid and turn to "Seal" position.
- Cook on "Manual" with "High Pressure" for about 30 minutes.
- Press the "Cancel" and allow a "Natural" release.
- Meanwhile, for curry: in a heavy bottomed skillet, heat the oil over medium heat and sauté mustard seeds for about 15-20 seconds.
- Add the onion and sauté for about 4-5 minutes.
- Add the ginger garlic paste, green chilies, curry leaves and spices and sauté for about 1 minute.
- Carefully, remove the lid of Instant Pot Mini and select "Sauté".
- Stir in the curry mixture and cook for about 4-5 minutes, stirring occasionally.
- Press the "Cancel" and serve hot.

Per Serving: Calories: 350; Total Fat: 18g; Saturated Fat: 11.6g; Protein: 36.3g; Carbs: 10.7g; Fiber: 3.5g; Sugar: 3.5g

Beef & Chickpeas Curry

Serves: 3 / Preparation time: 15 minutes / Cooking time: 30 minutes

2 tablespoons ghee

½ pound beef stew meat, cut into 1-inch cubes

½ teaspoon fresh ginger, grated

1 garlic clove, chopped finely

1 tablespoon curry powder

1 cup unsweetened coconut milk

Salt and ground black pepper, to taste

1½ cups canned chickpeas, rinsed and drained

- Add the ghee in the Instant Pot Mini and select "Sauté". Now, add the beef and cook for about 5-6 minutes.
- Add the ginger, garlic and curry powder and cook for about 1 minute.
- Press the "Cancel" and stir in the coconut milk, salt and black pepper.
- Secure the lid and turn to "Seal" position.
- Cook on "Manual" with "High Pressure" for about 20 minutes.
- Press the "Cancel" and allow a "Natural" release.
- Carefully, remove the lid and select "Sauté".
- Stir in the chickpeas and cook for about 5-10 minutes.
- Press the "Cancel" and serve hot.

Per Serving: Calories: 773; Total Fat: 38.6g; Saturated Fat: 24.7g; Protein: 44.4g; Carbs: 66.8g; Fiber: 19.9g; Sugar: 13.5g

Beef with Green Beans

Serves: 4 / Preparation time: 15 minutes / Cooking time: 30 minutes

For Spice Blend

1 tablespoon ground cinnamon

¾ teaspoon ground nutmeg

¼ teaspoon ground allspice

Salt and ground black pepper, to taste

For Beef Mixture

1 pound beef chuck roast, cut in 2-inch chunks

1 pound fresh green beans, trimmed and cut in 2-inch pieces

1 medium onion, chopped

32 ounces canned tomato sauce

- For spice blend: in a bowl, add all the ingredients and mix well.
- In the pot of Instant Pot Mini, place the spice blend and remaining all ingredients and stir to combine.
- Secure the lid and turn to "Seal" position.
- Select "Meat/Stew" and just use the default time of 30 minutes.
- Press the "Cancel" and allow a "Natural" release.
- Carefully, remove the lid and serve hot.

Per Serving: Calories: 520; Total Fat: 32.4g; Saturated Fat: 12.8g; Protein: 35.1g; Carbs: 24.6g; Fiber: 8.9g; Sugar: 12.6g

Beef with Broccoli

Serves: 4 / Preparation time: 15 minutes / Cooking time: 36 minutes

1 tablespoon olive oil

1 pound chuck roast beef, trimmed and cut into thin strips

Salt and ground black pepper, as required

1 small onion, chopped

2 garlic cloves, minced

Pinch of red pepper flakes, crushed

½ cup beef broth

¼ cup soy sauce

2 tablespoons brown sugar

1 tablespoon cornstarch

1½ tablespoons cold water

¾ pound broccoli florets

2 tablespoons water

2 tablespoons fresh cilantro, chopped

- Add the oil in an Instant Pot Mini and select "Sauté". Now, add the beef, salt and black pepper and cook for about 5 minutes or until browned completely.
- With a slotted spoon, transfer the beef into a bowl.
- In the pot, add the onion and cook for about 4-5 minutes.
- Add the garlic and red pepper flakes and cook for about 1 minute.
- Press the "Cancel" and stir in the beef, broth, soy sauce and brown sugar.
- Secure the lid and turn to "Seal" position.
- Cook on "Manual" with "High Pressure" for about 12 minutes.
- Press the "Cancel" and allow a "Quick" release.
- Meanwhile, in a bowl, add the cornstarch and cold water and mix until well combined.
- Carefully, remove the lid and add the cornstarch mixture, stirring continuously.
- Now, select "Sauté" and cook for about 4-5 minutes.
- Meanwhile, in a large microwave-safe bowl, add the broccoli and 2 tablespoons of water and microwave on High for 3-4 minutes or until broccoli becomes tender.
- Add the broccoli into the pot and stir well.
- Press the "Cancel" and serve hot.

Per Serving: Calories: 392; Total Fat: 18.9g; Saturated Fat: 6.3g; Protein: 39.5g; Carbs: 15.8g; Fiber: 2.8g; Sugar: 7g

Beef with Bell Peppers

Serves: 4 / Preparation time: 20 minutes / Cooking time: 32 minutes

1 tablespoon olive oil

1 pound boneless beef, trimmed and cut into thin strips

Salt and ground black pepper, as required

1½ cups canned tomato sauce

1 teaspoon dried thyme, crushed

1 large onion, cut into ½-inch thick strips

3 large bell peppers, seeded and cut into ½-inch thick strips

2 cups tomatoes, chopped finely

2 garlic cloves, minced

1 cup water

- Add the oil in an Instant Pot Mini and select "Sauté". Now, add the beef, salt and black pepper and cook for about 5-6 minutes or until browned completely
- With a slotted spoon, transfer the beef into a bowl.
- In the pot, add the tomatoes, tomato sauce, garlic, thyme, salt, black pepper and water and stir to combine.
- Press the "Cancel" and stir in the beef, onion and bell peppers.
- Secure the lid and turn to "Seal" position.
- Cook on "Manual" with "High Pressure" for about 25 minutes.
- Press the "Cancel" and allow a "Quick" release.
- Carefully, remove the lid and serve hot.

Per Serving: Calories: 325; Total Fat: 11.2g; Saturated Fat: 3.2g; Protein: 37.8g; Carbs: 19.4g; Fiber: 4.6g; Sugar: 12.4g

Honey Glazed Steak

Serves: 4 / Preparation time: 15 minutes / Cooking time: 23 minutes

½ tablespoon olive oil

1 pound flank steak, trimmed and cut into ¼-inch thick strips

Salt and ground black pepper, as required

2 garlic cloves, minced

¼ teaspoon fresh ginger, minced

¼ cup water

¼ cup soy sauce

2 tablespoons honey

1 tablespoon cornstarch

1½ tablespoons cold water

2 scallions, chopped

- Add the oil in an Instant Pot Mini and select "Sauté". Now, add the steak, salt and black pepper and cook for about 5 minutes or until browned completely.
- With a slotted spoon, transfer the steak into a bowl.
- In the pot, add the garlic and ginger and cook for about 1 minute.
- Press the "Cancel" and stir in the steak, ¼ cup of the water, soy sauce and honey.
- Secure the lid and turn to "Seal" position.
- Cook on "Manual" with "High Pressure" for about 12 minutes.
- Press the "Cancel" and allow a "Quick" release.
- Meanwhile, in a bowl, add the cornstarch and cold water and mix until well combined.
- Carefully, remove the lid and select "Sauté".
- Add the cornstarch mixture, stirring continuously.
- Cook for about 4-5 minutes, stirring continuously.
- Press the "Cancel" and stir in the scallion.
- Serve hot

Per Serving: Calories: 289; Total Fat: 11.2g; Saturated Fat: 4.2g; Protein: 32.8g; Carbs: 13.2g; Fiber: 0g; Sugar: 9.1g

Steak in Orange Sauce

Serves: 4 / Preparation time: 15 minutes / Cooking time: 23 minutes

1 tablespoon olive oil

1 pound flank steak, cut into ¼-inch thick strips

Salt and ground black pepper, as required

2 garlic cloves, minced

½ teaspoon fresh orange zest, grated

1/3 cup fresh orange juice

2 tablespoons soy sauce

¼ teaspoon red pepper flakes, crushed

1 tablespoons cornstarch

1 tablespoons water

- Add the oil in an Instant Pot Mini and select "Sauté". Now, add the steak, salt and black pepper and cook for about 5 minutes or until browned completely.
- Stir in the garlic and cook for about 1 minute.
- Press the "Cancel" and stir in the orange zest, orange juice, soy sauce and red pepper flakes.
- Secure the lid and turn to "Seal" position.
- Cook on "Manual" with "High Pressure" for about 12 minutes.
- Press the "Cancel" and allow a "Quick" release.
- Meanwhile, in a bowl, add the cornstarch and cold water and mix until well combined.
- Carefully, remove the lid and select "Sauté".
- Add the cornstarch mixture, stirring continuously.
- Cook for about 4-5 minutes, stirring continuously.
- Press the "Cancel" and serve hot

Per Serving: Calories: 274; Total Fat: 13g; Saturated Fat: 4.4g; Protein: 32.3g; Carbs: 5.2g; Fiber: 0g; Sugar: 1.9g

Steak with Salsa

Serves: 4 / Preparation time: 15 minutes / Cooking time: 8 hours

Nonstick cooking spray

1½ pounds beef round steak, cut in 2-inch strips

1 (14-ounce) can diced tomatoes

1 (8-ounce) can tomato sauce

3 ounces canned diced green chilies

3 tablespoons salsa

1½ tablespoons Mexican seasoning

Salt, to taste

¼ cup Cheddar cheese, grated

- Grease the pot of Instant Pot Mini with the cooking spray.
- In the prepared pot, place all the ingredients except the cheese and stir to combine.
- Secure the lid and turn to "Seal" position.
- Select the "Slow Cooker" with "Medium" settings for about 6-8 hours.
- Press the "Cancel" and carefully allow a "Natural" release.
- Press the "Cancel" and serve hot with the topping of Cheddar cheese.

Per Serving: Calories: 506; Total Fat: 19g; Saturated Fat: 7g; Protein: 60g; Carbs: 24.3g; Fiber: 8.3g; Sugar: 14.2g

Beef with Tuna Sauce

Serves: 4 / Preparation time: 20 minutes / Cooking time: 39 minutes

For Beef

2 tablespoons olive oil

1 pound beef chuck roast

1 onion, chopped finely

1 carrot, peeled and chopped finely

1 celery stalk, chopped finely

2 garlic cloves, minced

1 tablespoon fresh rosemary, chopped

4 bay leaves

Salt and ground black pepper, as required

1 cup water

1 cup white wine

For Sauce

1½ (5½-ounce) cans olive oil packed tuna, strained and divided

1 cup mayonnaise

3 anchovies

2 tablespoons capers

- Add the oil in an Instant Pot Mini and select "Sauté". Now, add the beef roast and cook for about 3-4 minutes per side.
- With a slotted spoon, transfer the roast into a bowl.
- In the pot, add the onion, carrot and celery and cook for about 5 minutes.
- Add the garlic, rosemary and bay leaves and cook for about 1 minute.
- Press the "Cancel" and stir in the roast, salt, black pepper, water and wine.
- Secure the lid and turn to "Seal" position.
- Cook on "Manual" with "High Pressure" for about 20-25 minutes.
- Press the "Cancel" and allow a "Natural" release.
- Carefully, remove the lid and transfer the roast onto a cutting board for about 5-10 minutes before slicing.
- Meanwhile, for sauce: in a food processor, add 1 can of tuna, mayonnaise and anchovies and pulse until smooth.
- Transfer the pureed sauce into a bowl.
- Add the remaining tuna and capers and stir to combine.
- Cut the roast into desired sized slices.
- Pour sauce over the roast slices and serve.

Per Serving: Calories: 928; Total Fat: 65.2g; Saturated Fat: 17.9g; Protein: 52.9g; Carbs: 20.9g; Fiber: 1.4g; Sugar: 6.2g

Coffee Braised Pulled Beef

Serves: 4 / Preparation time: 15 minutes / Cooking time: 35 minutes

For Beef Rub

2 tablespoons coffee, finely ground

1 tablespoon cocoa powder

1 tablespoon paprika

¾ teaspoon ground ginger

¾ teaspoon red chili powder

1 teaspoon red pepper flakes, crushed

Salt and ground black pepper, to taste

1½ pounds beef chuck roast, trimmed and cut into 1½-inch cubes

For Sauce

1 cup beef broth

½ cup brewed coffee

1 medium onion, chopped

2 tablespoons fresh lemon juice

Salt and ground black pepper, to taste

- For rub: in a small bowl, add all the ingredients except the roast and mix well.
- Rub the chuck roast with rub mixture generously.
- For sauce: in a food processor, add all the ingredients and pulse until smooth.
- In the pot of Instant Pot Mini, place the roast and top with sauce evenly.
- Secure the lid and turn to "Seal" position.
- Select "Meat/Stew" and just use the default time of 35 minutes.
- Press the "Cancel" and allow a "Natural" release.
- Carefully, remove the lid and transfer the roast onto a platter.
- With 2 forks, shred the meat.
- Top with the sauce and serve.

Per Serving: Calories: 653; Total Fat: 48.4g; Saturated Fat: 19.2g; Protein: 46.8g; Carbs: 5.6g; Fiber: 2.1g; Sugar: 1.8g

Ground Beef with Peas

Serves: 4 / Preparation time: 15 minutes / Cooking time: 22 minutes

2 tablespoons coconut oil	1 small onion, chopped finely
½ tablespoon ginger paste	½ tablespoon garlic paste
2 teaspoons garam masala powder	2 teaspoons ground coriander
1 teaspoon ground cumin	1 teaspoon paprika
½ teaspoon red chili powder	½ teaspoon ground turmeric
Salt, to taste	1 pound ground beef
3 tablespoons tomato paste	¾ cup water
1 cup frozen peas	2 tablespoons fresh cilantro, chopped

- Add the oil in an Instant Pot Mini and select "Sauté". Now, add the onion, ginger and garlic paste and cook for about 2-3 minutes.
- Add the spices and cook for about 1 minute.
- Add the beef and tomato paste and cook for about 4-5 minutes.
- Press the "Cancel" and stir in the water.
- Secure the lid and turn to "Seal" position.
- Cook on "Manual" with "High Pressure" for about 10 minutes.
- Press the "Cancel" and allow a "Quick" release.
- Carefully, remove the lid and select "Sauté".
- Stir in the peas and cook for about 2-3 minutes.
- Press the "Cancel" and stir in the cilantro.
- Serve hot.

Per Serving: Calories: 327; Total Fat: 14.4g; Saturated Fat: 8.6g; Protein: 37.6g; Carbs: 11.4g; Fiber: 3.6g; Sugar: 4.2g

Ground Beef with Cabbage & Rice

Serves: 4 / Preparation time: 15 minutes / Cooking time: 26 minutes

1 teaspoon olive oil

Salt, to taste

1 garlic clove, minced

Freshly ground black pepper, to taste

1 (8-ounce) can tomato sauce

½ teaspoon paprika

1 cup cooked brown rice

1 pound 93% lean ground beef

1 cup onion, chopped

1 tablespoon dried marjoram

1 cup beef broth

2 tablespoons raisins

1 medium head cabbage, chopped

- Add the oil in an Instant Pot Mini and select "Sauté". Now, add the beef and salt and cook for about 5 minutes.
- Add the onion, garlic, marjoram and black pepper and cook for about 2-3 minutes.
- Press the "Cancel" and stir in the broth, tomato sauce, raisins and paprika.
- Press the "Cancel" and stir in the water.
- Secure the lid and turn to "Seal" position.
- Cook on "Manual" with "High Pressure" for about 15 minutes.
- Press the "Cancel" and allow a "Quick" release.
- Carefully, remove the lid and mix in the cabbage and rice.
- Secure the lid and turn to "Seal" position.
- Cook on "Manual" with "High Pressure" for about 3 minutes.
- Press the "Cancel" and allow a "Quick" release.
- Carefully, remove the lid and serve hot.

Per Serving: Calories: 448; Total Fat: 11.2g; Saturated Fat: 3.6g; Protein: 32.4g; Carbs: 56.8g; Fiber: 8g; Sugar: 12.3g

Ground Beef with Veggies & Oats

Serves: 4 / Preparation time: 20 minutes / Cooking time: 28 minutes

1 tablespoon olive oil

1 medium bell pepper, seeded and chopped

1 carrot, peeled and grated

1 cup canned chopped tomatoes with liquid

¼ cup apple cider vinegar

1 tablespoon Worcestershire sauce

½ cup rolled oats

1 pound lean ground beef

1 medium onion, chopped

2 teaspoons garlic powder

¼ cup canned tomato sauce

1 cup water

Salt and ground black pepper, to taste

- Add the oil in an Instant Pot Mini and select "Sauté". Now, add the beef and cook for about 6-8 minutes or until browned.
- Add the bell pepper, onion and carrot and cook for about 4-5 minutes.
- Press the "Cancel" and stir in the remaining ingredients except the oats.
- Place the oats on top.
- Secure the lid and turn to "Seal" position.
- Cook on "Manual" with "High Pressure" for about 10 minutes.
- Press the "Cancel" and allow a "Natural" release.
- Carefully, remove the lid and select "Sauté".
- Cook for about 5 minutes or until all the liquid is absorbed.
- Press the "Cancel" and serve.

Per Serving: Calories: 330; Total Fat: 11.5g; Saturated Fat: 3.3g; Protein: 37.3g; Carbs: 17.7g; Fiber: 3.3g; Sugar: 6.5g

Beef Lasagna

Serves: 4 / Preparation time: 20 minutes / Cooking time: 34 minutes

2 tablespoons olive oil

1 teaspoon dried thyme, crushed

Salt and ground black pepper, as required

1 medium carrot, peeled and chopped finely

2 tablespoons fresh rosemary, chopped

8 ounces lasagna noodles, broken into 2-inch pieces

1 cup water

3 garlic cloves, minced

1 pound lean ground beef

1 medium onion, chopped finely

1 celery stalk, chopped finely

1 cup tomato puree

4 ounces mozzarella cheese, grated

- Add the oil in an Instant Pot Mini and select "Sauté". Now, add the garlic and thyme and cook for about 1 minute.
- Add the beef, salt and black pepper and cook for about 5 minutes or until browned.
- With a slotted spoon, transfer the beef into a bowl.
- In the pot, add the onion, carrot, celery and rosemary and cook for about 5 minutes.
- Press the "Cancel" and stir in the cooked beef and tomato puree.
- Secure the lid and turn to "Seal" position.
- Cook on "Manual" with "High Pressure" for about 18 minutes.
- Press the "Cancel" and allow a "Quick" release.
- Carefully, remove the lid and add the lasagna noodles with a little salt.
- Pour water on top and with the back of spoon, slightly press the noodles.
- Secure the lid and turn to "Seal" position.
- Cook on "Manual" with "High Pressure" for about 5 minutes.
- Press the "Cancel" and allow a "Quick" release.
- Carefully, remove the lid and serve with the sprinkling of the cheese.

Per Serving: Calories: 561; Total Fat: 20.5g; Saturated Fat: 6.8g; Protein: 50.7g; Carbs: 43.7g; Fiber: 3g; Sugar: 5g

Sweet & Sour Meatballs

Serves: 4 / Preparation time: 15 minutes / Cooking time: 10 minutes

1 pound extra-lean ground beef

2/3 cup pineapple juice

¼ cup brown sugar

1 tablespoon soy sauce

1 egg

¼ cup vinegar

3 tablespoons tomato paste

- In a bowl, add the beef and egg and mix well.
- Make 1-inch meatballs from the mixture.
- In a bowl, add the remaining ingredients and beat until well combined.
- In the pot of Instant Pot Mini, place the meatballs and top with the sauce evenly.
- Secure the lid and turn to "Seal" position.
- Cook on "Manual" with "High Pressure" for about 10 minutes.
- Press the "Cancel" and allow a "Natural" release for about 5 minutes and then allow a "Quick" release.
- Carefully, remove the lid and gently, stir the mixture.
- Serve hot.

Per Serving: Calories: 306; Total Fat: 9.8g; Saturated Fat: 4.3g; Protein: 35.4g; Carbs: 17g; Fiber: 0.6g; Sugar: 14.6g

Cheese Stuffed Beef Burgers

Serves: 2 / Preparation time: 15 minutes / Cooking time: 5 minutes

1 pound ground beef

Salt and ground black pepper, as required

1 tablespoon Worcestershire sauce

2 ounces Cheddar cheese, shredded

- Add the oil in an Instant Pot Mini and select "Sauté". Now, add the cumin seeds and cook for about 30 seconds.
- In a large bowl, add the ground beef, Worcestershire Sauce, salt and black pepper and mix until well combined.
- Make 4 equal sized balls from the mixture and with your hands, fatten each ball.
- Place 1 ounce of the cheese in the center of 2 of the flattened balls.
- Cover each with remaining 2 flattened balls, pressing the edges together well.
- Arrange a steamer tray in the bottom of an Instant Pot Mini and pour ½ cup of water.
- Place burgers on top of the steamer tray.
- Secure the lid and turn to "Seal" position.
- Cook on "Manual" with "High Pressure" for about 5 minutes.
- Press the "Cancel" and allow a "Natural" release.
- Carefully, remove the lid and serve.

Per Serving: Calories: 543; Total Fat: 23.5g; Saturated Fat: 11.3g; Protein: 75.9g; Carbs: 1.9g; Fiber: 0g; Sugar: 1.7g

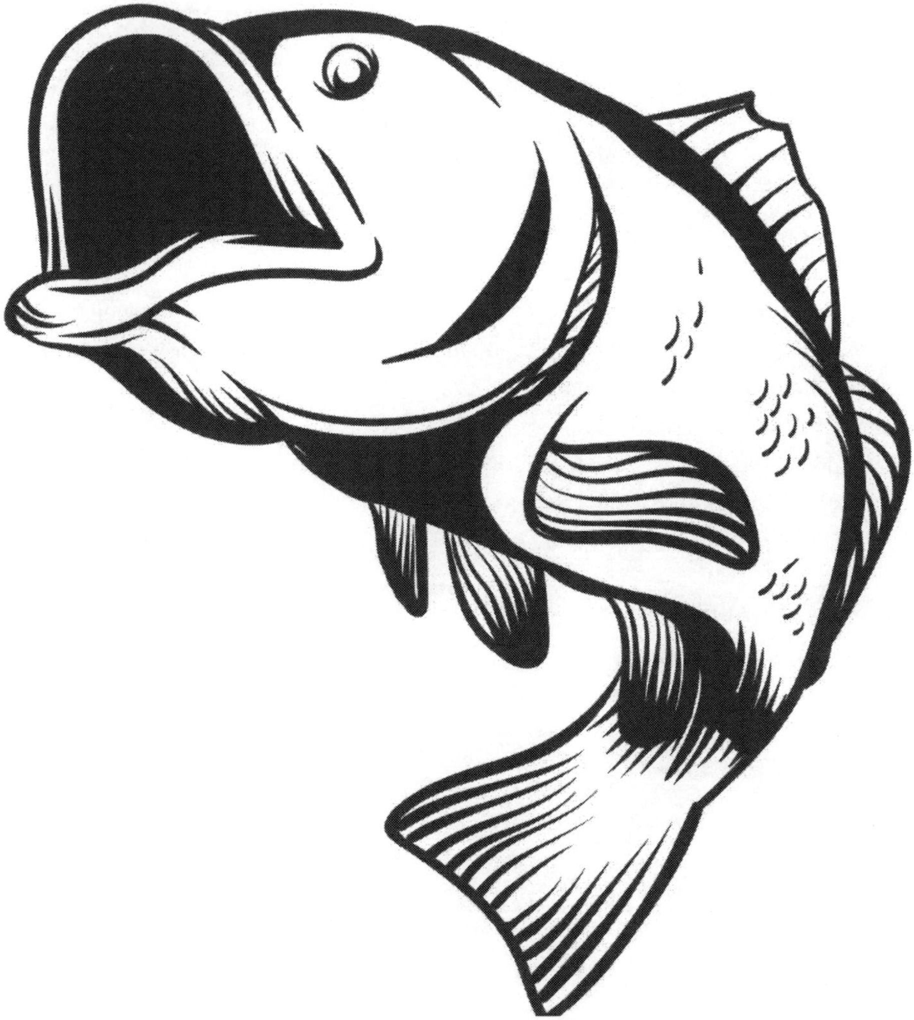

SEAFOOD RECIPES

Contents

Haddock Soup	90
Clam Soup	91
Seafood Stew	92
Catfish Curry	93
Salmon Curry	94
Citrus Salmon	95
Salmon in Green Sauce	96
Salmon in Creamy Sauce	97
Salmon Casserole	98
Sweet & Sour Mahi-Mahi	99
Cod with Tomatoes	100
Cod with Peas	101
Cod Parcel	102
Shrimp with Potatoes	103
Shrimp with Green Beans	104
Shrimp with Rice	105
Calamari with Tomatoes	106
Lemony Mussels	107
Steamed Lobster Tails	108
Buttered Crab Legs	109

Haddock Soup

Serves: 4 / Preparation time: 15 minutes / Cooking time: 16 minutes

2 tablespoons butter

1 celery stalk, chopped

1 carrot, peeled and chopped

¾ pound haddock fillets

1 cup frozen corn

3½ cups chicken broth

1 tablespoon cornstarch

½ cup bacon, chopped

1 onion, chopped

2 garlic cloves, chopped finely

2 cups potatoes, cubed

2 cups heavy cream

Salt and ground white pepper, to taste

- Add the butter in the Instant Pot Mini and select "Sauté". Now, add the bacon and cook for about 4-5 minutes.
- Add the celery, onion, carrot and garlic and cook for about 3 minutes.
- Press the "Cancel" and stir in the remaining ingredients.
- Secure the lid and turn to "Seal" position.
- Cook on "Manual" with "High Pressure" for about 5 minutes.
- Press the "Cancel" and allow a "Natural" release.
- Carefully, remove the lid and select "Sauté".
- Cook for about 3 minutes.
- Press the "Cancel" and serve hot.

Per Serving: Calories: 768; Total Fat: 46.5g; Saturated Fat: 23.1g; Protein: 54.3g; Carbs: 31.2g; Fiber: 3.9g; Sugar: 6.9g

Clam Soup

Serves: 4 / Preparation time: 20 minutes / Cooking time: 23 minutes

- 1 teaspoon olive oil
- 1 medium onion, chopped finely
- ½ cup white wine
- 2 cups clam juice
- 1 bay leaf
- 1 tablespoon flour
- 11 ounces canned clams, strained
- 1 cup milk
- 4 bacon slices
- Salt and ground black pepper, to taste
- 2 medium potatoes, cubed
- 2 tablespoons fresh thyme, chopped
- Pinch of cayenne pepper
- 1 tablespoon butter, melted
- 1 cup cream

- Add the oil in an Instant Pot Mini and select "Sauté". Now, add the bacon and cook for about 5 minutes.
- Add the onion, salt and black pepper and cook for about 5 minutes.
- Stir in the wine and cook for about 2-3 minutes.
- Press the "Cancel" and stir in the potatoes, clam juice, thyme, bay leaf and cayenne pepper.
- Secure the lid and turn to "Seal" position.
- Cook on "Manual" with "High Pressure" for about 5 minutes.
- Press the "Cancel" and allow a "Natural" release.
- Meanwhile in a small pan, mix together the flour and butter over medium-low heat and cook for about 2 minutes, stirring continuously.
- Carefully, remove the lid and select "Sauté".
- Add the flour mixture, clam meat, cream and milk and stir to combine.
- Cook for about 5 minutes, stirring occasionally.
- Press the "Cancel" and serve hot.

Per Serving: Calories: 472; Total Fat: 21g; Saturated Fat: 8.7g; Protein: 16.5g; Carbs: 49.7g; Fiber: 4.6g; Sugar: 13.2g

Seafood Stew

Serves: 4 / Preparation time: 25 minutes / Cooking time: 15 minutes

3 tablespoons olive oil

2 bay leaves

1 small bell pepper, seeded and sliced thinly

2 garlic cloves, minced

Salt and ground black pepper, to taste

12 Little neck clams

¾ pound cod fillets, cut into 2-inch chunks

2 teaspoons paprika

1½ cups tomatoes, chopped

1 small onion, sliced thinly

1 cup fish broth

¾ pound shrimp, peeled and deveined

¼ cup fresh parsley, chopped

- Add the oil in an Instant Pot Mini and select "Sauté". Now, add the paprika and bay leaves and cook for about 30 seconds.
- Add the tomatoes, bell pepper, onion and garlic and cook for about 3-4 minutes.
- Press the "Cancel" and stir in the broth, salt and black pepper.
- Place the shrimp and clams on top and gently, submerge in broth mixture.
- Arrange the cod pieces on top.
- Secure the lid and turn to "Seal" position.
- Cook on "Manual" with "High Pressure" for about 10 minutes.
- Press the "Cancel" and allow a "Natural" release for about 10 minutes and then allow a "Quick" release.
- Carefully, remove the lid and serve hot with the garnishing of parsley.

Per Serving: Calories: 328; Total Fat: 13.6g; Saturated Fat: 2.2g; Protein: 42g; Carbs: 9.2g; Fiber: 2.1g; Sugar: 4.2g

Catfish Curry

Serves: 4 / Preparation time: 20 minutes / Cooking time: 12 minutes

For Fish Marinade
1 pound catfish, cut into pieces
½ teaspoon garlic paste
1 teaspoon ground coriander
½ teaspoon ground turmeric
½ teaspoon ginger paste
1 teaspoon red chili powder
1 teaspoon garam masala

For Curry Paste
1 tablespoon ghee
½ teaspoon ginger paste
2 tomatoes, chopped
½ teaspoon red chili powder
¼ cup fish broth
,1 onion, chopped
½ teaspoon garlic paste
2 teaspoons curry powder
Salt and ground black pepper, to taste
½ cup coconut milk

- For marinade: place all the ingredients in a large bowl and mix well.
- Refrigerate to marinate for about 30 minutes.
- Add the oil in an Instant Pot Mini and select "Sauté". Now, add the onions and cook for about 3-4 minutes.
- Add the ginger garlic paste and spices and cook for about 1 minute.
- Add the tomatoes and cook for about 2 minutes.
- Press the "Cancel" and with an immersion blender, blend until smooth.
- Stir in the fish, broth and coconut milk.
- Secure the lid and turn to "Seal" position.
- Cook on "Manual" with "Low Pressure" for about 5 minutes.
- Press the "Cancel" and allow a "Natural" release.
- Carefully, remove the lid and mix in the lemon juice.
- Serve hot.

Per Serving: Calories: 344; Total Fat: 25.1g; Saturated Fat: 16.7g; Protein: 24.3g; Carbs: 9g; Fiber: 2.8g; Sugar: 4.2g

Salmon Curry

Serves: 4 / Preparation time: 15 minutes / Cooking time: 11 minutes

1 tablespoon coconut oil

1 teaspoon fresh ginger, grated

1 Serrano pepper, chopped

1 teaspoon red chili powder

1 teaspoon ground coriander

1 cup unsweetened coconut milk

1 medium tomato, chopped finely

1 tablespoon fresh lime juice

1 medium onion, chopped

3 garlic cloves, minced

2 curry leaves

1 teaspoon ground cumin

¼ teaspoon ground turmeric

1 pound salmon fillets, cubed

Salt, to taste

- Add the oil in an Instant Pot Mini and select "Sauté". Now, add the onion and cook for about 5 minutes.
- Add the ginger, garlic, Serrano pepper and spices and cook for about 1 minute.
- Press the "Cancel" and stir in the coconut milk, salmon, tomatoes and salt.
- Secure the lid and turn to "Seal" position.
- Cook on "Manual" with "Low Pressure" for about 5 minutes.
- Press the "Cancel" and allow a "Quick" release.
- Carefully, remove the lid and mix in the lime juice.
- Serve hot.

Per Serving: Calories: 344; Total Fat: 25.1g; Saturated Fat: 16.7g; Protein: 24.3g; Carbs: 9g; Fiber: 2.8g; Sugar: 4.2g

Citrus Salmon

Serves: 4 / Preparation time: 15 minutes / Cooking time: 7 minutes

4 (4-ounce) salmon fillets

2 teaspoons fresh orange zest, grated finely

1 tablespoon olive oil

Salt and ground black pepper, to taste

1 teaspoon fresh ginger, minced

1 cup white wine

3 tablespoons fresh orange juice

- Add the oil in an Instant Pot Mini and select "Sauté". Now, add the cumin seeds and cook for about 30 seconds.
- In the pot of Instant Pot Mini, add all the ingredients and stir to combine.
- Secure the lid and turn to "Seal" position.
- Cook on "Manual" with "High Pressure" for about 7 minutes.
- Press the "Cancel" and carefully allow a "Natural" release.
- Carefully, remove the lid and serve the salmon fillets with the topping of cooking sauce.

Per Serving: Calories: 237; Total Fat: 10.6g; Saturated Fat: 1.5g; Protein: 22.2g; Carbs: 3.4g; Fiber: 0g; Sugar: 1.5g

Salmon in Green Sauce

Serves: 4 / Preparation time: 15 minutes / Cooking time: 12 minutes

Nonstick cooking spray

3 garlic cloves, chopped

1 tablespoon capers

1 tablespoon fresh lemon zest, grated finely

½ cup water

1 avocado, peeled, pitted and chopped

½ cup fresh basil, chopped

4 (6-ounce) salmon fillets

- Grease a large piece of the foil.
- Place all the ingredients in a large bowl except the salmon and water and with a fork, mash completely.
- Place the salmon fillets in the center of foil and top with the avocado mixture evenly.
- Fold the foil around the salmon fillets to seal it.
- Arrange a steamer trivet in the bottom of an Instant Pot Mini and pour ½ cup of the water.
- Place the foil packet on top of the trivet.
- Secure the lid and turn to "Seal" position.
- Cook on "Manual" with "High Pressure" for about 8 minutes.
- Press the "Cancel" and carefully allow a "Natural" release.
- Meanwhile, preheat the oven to broiler.
- Carefully, remove the lid and transfer the salmon fillets onto a broiler pan.
- Broil for about 3-4 minutes.
- Serve warm.

Per Serving: Calories: 333; Total Fat: 20.4g; Saturated Fat: 3.6g; Protein: 34.3g; Carbs: 5.6g; Fiber: 3.6g; Sugar: 0g

Salmon in Creamy Sauce

Serves: 4 / Preparation time: 15 minutes / Cooking time: 3 minutes

For Sauce

¾ cup mayonnaise	¾ cup plain Greek yogurt
¼ cup scallion, chopped	1/3 cup dill pickle relish
3 tablespoons fresh parsley, chopped	
3 tablespoons capers, drained and chopped	1 teaspoon Dijon mustard

Salt and freshly ground black pepper, as required

For Salmon

1 medium onion, sliced	4 (4-ounce) salmon fillets
¾ cup dry white wine	1 teaspoon dried dill weed
Salt and ground black pepper, as required	1 lemon, sliced

1 cup water

- In a large bowl, add oil, lemon juice, garlic, feta, oregano, salt and black pepper and beat until well combined.
- Arrange a steamer trivet in the bottom of an Instant Pot Mini and pour 1½ cups of the water.
- Place the salmon fillets on top of the trivet in a single layer and top with the dressing.
- Arrange 1 rosemary sprig and 1 lemon slice over each fillet.
- Secure the lid and turn to "Seal" position.
- Select "Steam" and just use the default time of 3 minutes.
- Press the "Cancel" and carefully allow a "Quick" release.
- Carefully, remove the lid and serve hot.

Per Serving: Calories: 428; Total Fat: 22g; Saturated Fat: 3.2g; Protein: 25.6g; Carbs: 27g; Fiber: 2g; Sugar: 14g

Salmon Casserole

Serves: 4 / Preparation time: 15 minutes / Cooking time: 9 hours

Nonstick cooking spray

¼ cup water

Salt and ground black pepper, to taste

1 (16-ounce) can salmon, drained and flaked

Pinch of ground nutmeg

10 ounces cream of mushroom soup

3 medium potatoes, peeled and sliced

3 tablespoons flour

½ cup scallion, chopped

- Grease the pot of Instant Pot Mini with the cooking spray.
- In a bowl, mix together the mushroom soup and water.
- In the prepared pot, place half of the potato slices and sprinkle with the salt and black pepper slightly and followed by half of the flour.
- Top with half of the salmon, followed by half of the scallion.
- Repeat the layers and top with the mushroom soup mixture.
- Sprinkle with the nutmeg evenly.
- Secure the lid and turn to "Seal" position.
- Select the "Slow Cooker" with "Medium" settings for about 7-9 hours.
- Press the "Cancel" and carefully allow a "Natural" release.
- Carefully, remove the lid and serve warm.

Per Serving: Calories: 316; Total Fat: 9.3g; Saturated Fat: 1.6g; Protein: 26.1g; Carbs: 32.9g; Fiber: 4.3g; Sugar: 2.7g

Sweet & Sour Mahi-Mahi

Serves: 2 / Preparation time: 15 minutes / Cooking time: 5 minutes

2 (4-ounce) mahi-mahi fillets

2 garlic cloves, minced

2 tablespoons honey

Salt and ground black pepper, to taste

2 tablespoons fresh lime juice

1 teaspoon red pepper flakes, crushed

- Season the mahi-mahi with salt and black pepper evenly.
- In a bowl, mix together remaining ingredients.
- Arrange a steamer trivet in the bottom of an Instant Pot Mini and pour 1 cup of the water.
- Place the fish fillets on top of trivet in a single layer and top with sauce.
- Secure the lid and turn to "Seal" position.
- Select "Steam" and just use the default time of 5 minutes.
- Press the "Cancel" and carefully allow a "Quick" release.
- Carefully, remove the lid and serve hot.

Per Serving: Calories: 162; Total Fat: 0.2g; Saturated Fat: 0g; Protein: 21.4g; Carbs: 18.9g; Fiber: 0.3g; Sugar: 17.4g

Cod with Tomatoes

Serves: 4 / Preparation time: 15 minutes / Cooking time: 5 minutes

1 pound cherry tomatoes, halved

4 (4-ounce) cod fillets

1 tablespoon olive oil

2 tablespoons fresh thyme

2 garlic cloves, minced

Salt and ground black pepper, to taste

- In the bottom of a greased a large heatproof bowl, place half of the cherry tomatoes, followed by the rosemary.
- Arrange cod fillets on top in a single layer, followed by the remaining tomatoes.
- Sprinkle with the garlic and drizzle with the oil.
- Arrange the bowl into the bottom of an Instant Pot Mini.
- Secure the lid and turn to "Seal" position.
- Cook on "Manual" with "High Pressure" for about 5 minutes.
- Press the "Cancel" and allow a "Quick" release.
- Carefully, remove the lid and transfer the fish fillets and tomatoes onto serving plates.
- Sprinkle with the salt and black pepper and serve.

Per Serving: Calories: 148; Total Fat: 4.8g; Saturated Fat: 0.6g; Protein: 21.5g; Carbs: 5.8g; Fiber: 1.9g; Sugar: 3g

Cod with Peas

Serves: 4 / Preparation time: 15 minutes / Cooking time: 4 minutes

4 (4-ounce) cod fillets

2 tablespoons fresh parsley

½ teaspoon paprika

½ pound frozen peas

2 garlic cloves, chopped

1 cup wine

- Add the oil in an Instant Pot Mini and select "Sauté". Now, add the cumin seeds and cook for about 30 seconds.
- Arrange a steamer trivet in the bottom of an Instant Pot Mini and pour 1 cup of the water.
- Arrange the cod fillets on top of the trivet.
- Secure the lid and turn to "Seal" position.
- Cook on "Manual" with "High Pressure" for about 2 minutes.
- Press the "Cancel" and allow a "Quick" release.
- Carefully, remove the lid and place the peas in the Instant Pot Mini.
- Secure the lid and turn to "Seal" position.
- Cook on "Manual" with "High Pressure" for about 2 minutes.
- Press the "Cancel" and allow a "Quick" release.
- Meanwhile, in a food processor, add the remaining ingredients and pulse until smooth.
- Transfer the parsley mixture into a bowl.
- Carefully, remove the lid and transfer the cod and peas into a bowl.
- Add the parsley mixture and stir to combine.
- Serve immediately.

Per Serving: Calories: 188; Total Fat: 1.2g; Saturated Fat: 0g; Protein: 23.4g; Carbs: 10.4g; Fiber: 3.3g; Sugar: 3.2g

Cod Parcel

Serves: 2 / Preparation time: 15 minutes / Cooking time: 2 minutes

2 (4-ounce) cod fillets

Salt and ground black pepper, as required

4 lemon slices

½ teaspoon garlic powder

2 fresh dill sprigs

2 tablespoons butter

- Arrange 2 large parchment squares onto a smooth surface.
- Place 1 cod fillet in the center of each parchment square and sprinkle with garlic powder, salt and black pepper.
- Top each fillet with 1 dill sprig, 2 lemon slices and 1 tablespoon of the butter.
- Fold each parchment paper around the fillets to seal.
- Arrange a steamer trivet in the bottom of an Instant Pot Mini and pour 1 cup of the water.
- Arrange the fish parcels on top of the trivet in a single layer.
- Secure the lid and turn to "Seal" position.
- Cook on "Manual" with "High Pressure" for about 2 minutes.
- Press the "Cancel" and allow a "Quick" release.
- Carefully, remove the lid and transfer fish parcels onto serving plates.
- Unwrap the parcels and serve.

Per Serving: Calories: 197; Total Fat: 12.6g; Saturated Fat: 7.3g; Protein: 20.6g; Carbs: 1g; Fiber: 0.2g; Sugar: 0.2g

Shrimp with Potatoes

Serves: 4 / Preparation time: 20 minutes / Cooking time: 9 minutes

1½ tablespoons canola oil

1 teaspoon ground cumin

1 teaspoon ground turmeric

2 medium white rose potatoes, cubed

¼ cup water

1¼ pounds medium shrimp, peeled and deveined

¼ cup fresh cilantro, chopped

1 medium onion, chopped

1½ teaspoons red chili powder

Salt, to taste

4 medium tomatoes, chopped

- Add the oil in an Instant Pot Mini and select "Sauté". Now, add the onion and cook for about 2-3 minutes.
- Add the spices and cook for about 1 minute.
- Add the potatoes and tomatoes and cook for about 2 minutes.
- Add the water and bring to a gentle simmer.
- Press the "Cancel" and stir in the shrimp.
- Secure the lid and turn to "Seal" position.
- Cook on "Manual" with "High Pressure" for about 3 minutes.
- Press the "Cancel" and allow a "Natural" release.
- Carefully, remove the lid and serve with the garnishing of cilantro.

Per Serving: Calories: 295; Total Fat: 7.7g; Saturated Fat: 0.5g; Protein: 33.8g; Carbs: 25.3g; Fiber: 5.2g; Sugar: 5.7g

Shrimp with Green Beans

Serves: 4 / Preparation time: 20 minutes / Cooking time: 2 minutes

¾ pound fresh green beans, trimmed

1 pound medium frozen shrimp, peeled and deveined

1 tablespoon butter, melted

2 tablespoons fresh lemon juice

Salt and ground black pepper, to taste

- Arrange a steamer trivet in the bottom of an Instant Pot Mini and pour 1 cup of the water.
- Arrange green beans on top of the trivet in a single layer and top with the shrimp.
- Drizzle with melted butter and lemon juice.
- Sprinkle with salt and black pepper.
- Secure the lid and turn to "Seal" position.
- Select "Steam" and just use the default time of 2 minutes.
- Press the "Cancel" and allow a "Natural" release.
- Carefully, remove the lid and serve.

Per Serving: Calories: 188; Total Fat: 5g; Saturated Fat: 2.5g; Protein: 27.5g; Carbs: 7.9g; Fiber: 2.9g; Sugar: 1.4g

Shrimp with Rice

Serves: 4 / Preparation time: 20 minutes / Cooking time: 17 minutes

1 tablespoon olive oil

1½ pounds shrimp, peeled and deveined

¼ teaspoon red pepper flakes, crushed and divided

Salt and ground black pepper, as required

1 small onion, chopped

1 large bell pepper, seeded and chopped

2 celery stalks, chopped

2 garlic cloves, minced

1 jalapeño pepper, seeded and chopped

2 cups tomatoes, chopped very finely

1 cup long grain white rice

1 cup chicken broth

¼ cup scallion (green part), chopped

- Add the oil in an Instant Pot Mini and select "Sauté". Now, add the shrimp, ¼ teaspoon of the red pepper flakes, salt and black pepper and cook for about 3 minutes.
- With a slotted spoon, transfer the shrimp into a bowl.
- In the pot, add the onion, bell pepper and celery and cook for about 5 minutes.
- Add the garlic, jalapeño, remaining red pepper flakes, salt and black pepper and cook for about 1 minute.
- Press the "Cancel" and stir in the tomatoes, rice and broth.
- Press the "Cancel" and stir in the shrimp.
- Secure the lid and turn to "Seal" position.
- Cook on "Manual" with "High Pressure" for about 8 minutes.
- Press the "Cancel" and allow a "Quick" release.
- Carefully, remove the lid and mix in the cooked shrimp.
- Immediately, secure the lid and turn to "Seal" position for about 5 minutes before serving.

Per Serving: Calories: 453; Total Fat: 7.4g; Saturated Fat: 1.g; Protein: 45g; Carbs: 48.9g; Fiber: 3.4g; Sugar: 5.5g

Calamari with Tomatoes

Serves: 4 / Preparation time: 15 minutes / Cooking time: 27minutes

2 tablespoons canola oil

1 teaspoon curry powder

1½ pounds fresh calamari, cleaned

1 cup chicken broth

Salt and ground black pepper, to taste

2 small garlic cloves, smashed

½ teaspoon red pepper flakes

1 (14½-ounce) can diced tomatoes

2 tablespoons fresh lemon juice

- Add the oil in an Instant Pot Mini and select "Sauté". Now, add the garlic, curry powder and red pepper flakes and cook for about 1 minute.
- Add the calamari and cook for about 5-6 minutes.
- Press the "Cancel" and stir in remaining ingredients.
- Secure the lid and turn to "Seal" position.
- Cook on "Manual" with "High Pressure" for about 20 minutes.
- Press the "Cancel" and allow a "Quick" release.
- Carefully, remove the lid and serve hot.

Per Serving: Calories: 135; Total Fat: 8.5g; Saturated Fat: 1.2g; Protein: 8.7g; Carbs: 6.2g; Fiber: 1.5g; Sugar: 3.1g

Lemony Mussels

Serves: 4 / Preparation time: 15 minutes / Cooking time: 7 minutes

1 tablespoon canola oil

1 garlic clove, minced

1 cup chicken broth

Salt and ground black pepper, to taste

2 pounds mussels, cleaned and de-bearded

1 onion, chopped

½ teaspoon dried rosemary, crushed

2 tablespoons fresh lemon juice

- Add the oil in an Instant Pot Mini and select "Sauté". Now, add the onion and cook for about 5 minutes.
- Add the garlic and rosemary and cook for about 1 minute.
- Press the "Cancel" and stir in the broth, lemon juice, salt and black pepper.
- Arrange steamer trivet in the Instant Pot.
- Place the mussels on top of the steamer trivet.
- Secure the lid and turn to "Seal" position.
- Cook on "Manual" with "Low Pressure" for about 1 minute.
- Press the "Cancel" and allow a "Quick" release.
- Carefully, remove the lid and transfer the mussels into a serving bowl.
- Top with the cooking liquid and serve.

Per Serving: Calories: 249; Total Fat: 9g; Saturated Fat: 1.6g; Protein: 28.6g; Carbs: 11.7g; Fiber: 0.7g; Sugar: 1.5g

Steamed Lobster Tails

Serves: 3 / Preparation time: 15 minutes / Cooking time: 3 minutes

2 pounds lobster tails, cut in half

2 tablespoons butter, melted

Salt, to taste

- Arrange a steamer trivet in the bottom of Instant Pot Mini and pour 1 cup of the water.
- Arrange the lobster tails on top of the trivet, shell side down.
- Secure the lid and turn to "Seal" position.
- Cook on "Manual" with "Low Pressure" for about 3 minutes.
- Press the "Cancel" and allow a "Quick" release.
- Carefully, remove the lid and transfer the tails onto a serving plate.
- Drizzle with the butter and sprinkle with the salt.
- Serve hot.

Per Serving: Calories: 338; Total Fat: 10.2g; Saturated Fat: 5.5g; Protein: 57.5g; Carbs: 0g; Fiber: 0g; Sugar: 0g

Buttered Crab Legs

Serves: 4 / Preparation time: 15 minutes / Cooking time: 4 minutes

1½ pounds frozen crab legs

2 tablespoons butter, melted

Salt, to taste

- Arrange a steamer trivet in the bottom of an Instant Pot Mini and pour 1 cup of the water alongside 1 teaspoon of the salt.
- Arrange the crab legs on top of the trivet and sprinkle with salt.
- Secure the lid and turn to "Seal" position.
- Cook on "Manual" with "High Pressure" for about 4 minutes.
- Press the "Cancel" and allow a "Quick" release.
- Carefully, remove the lid and transfer the crab legs onto a serving platter.
- Drizzle with the butter and serve.

Per Serving: Calories: 223; Total Fat: 8.3g; Saturated Fat: 3.7g; Protein: 32.7g; Carbs: 0g; Fiber: 0g; Sugar: 0g

VEGETABLE RECIPES

Contents

Beet Salad 112
Creamy Potato Salad 113
Onion Soup 114
Creamy Mushrooms 115
Mushrooms with Zucchini 116
Spinach in Tomato Sauce 117
Garlicky Bok Choy 118
Kale with Carrots 119
Stuffed Eggplants 120
Stuffed Spicy Potatoes 121
Potatoes with Peas 122
Peas with Cottage Cheese 123
Jackfruit Curry 124
Cauliflower Rice 125

Beet Salad

Serves: 2 / Preparation time: 20 minutes / Cooking time: 25 minutes

For Salad

4 medium red beets, trimmed and peeled

1 tablespoon white vinegar

¼ cup walnuts, chopped

For Dressing

2 garlic cloves, minced

2 tablespoons extra-virgin olive oil

Salt and ground black pepper, as required

4 cups mixed fresh greens

¼ cup feta cheese, crumbled

2 tablespoons fresh cilantro, minced

- Arrange a steamer trivet in the bottom of an Instant Pot Mini and pour 1 cup of the water.
- Place the beets on top of the trivet in a single layer.
- Secure the lid and turn to "Seal" position.
- Cook on "Manual" with "High Pressure" for about 25 minutes.
- Press the "Cancel" and allow a "Quick" release.
- Carefully, remove the lid and transfer the beet into a colander.
- Rinse the beets under the running cold water.
- Cut the beets in desired size slices and transfer into a salad bowl.
- Add salad greens and drizzle with vinegar.
- Meanwhile, in a bowl, add all the dressing ingredients and beat until well combined.
- Place the dressing over the beets mixture and gently toss to coat well.
- Serve immediately with the topping of cheese.

Per Serving: Calories: 196; Total Fat: 14.4g; Saturated Fat: 3g; Protein: 6.3g; Carbs: 13.6g; Fiber: 4g; Sugar: 7.3g

Creamy Potato Salad

Serves: 4 / Preparation time: 15 minutes / Cooking time: 4 minutes

For Salad

6 medium russet potatoes, peeled and cubed   4 large eggs

For Dressing

1 cup cream   1 tablespoon Dijon mustard

¼ cup red onion, chopped finely   2 tablespoons fresh cilantro, minced

Salt and ground black pepper, to taste   2 scallions (green part), chopped

- Arrange a steamer trivet in the bottom of an Instant Pot Mini and pour 1½ cups the water.
- Place potatoes and eggs on top of the trivet in a single layer.
- Secure the lid and turn to "Seal" position.
- Cook on "Manual" with "High Pressure" for about 4 minutes.
- Press the "Cancel" and allow a "Quick" release.
- Carefully, remove the lid and place the potatoes into a large bowl.
- Transfer the eggs into a bowl of the chilled water.
- Peel the eggs and then, chop them.
- Add the eggs into the bowl with potatoes.
- In another bowl, add all the dressing ingredients and beat until well combined.
- Place the dressing over the salad and stir to combine.
- Top with scallion and serve immediately.

Per Serving: Calories: 339; Total Fat: 8.8g; Saturated Fat: 3.7g; Protein: 12.5g; Carbs: 53.9g; Fiber: 8.2g; Sugar: 5.8g

Onion Soup

Serves: 4 / Preparation time: 15 minutes / Cooking time: 13 minutes

¼ cup unsalted butter

4 cups vegetable broth

¼ cup Gruyere cheese, shredded

5 onions, sliced

Salt and ground black pepper, to taste

- Add the butter in the Instant Pot Mini and select "Sauté". Now, add the onion and cook for about 3 minutes.
- Press the "Cancel" and stir in the broth, salt and black pepper.
- Secure the lid and turn to "Seal" position.
- Cook on "Manual" with "High Pressure" for about 10 minutes.
- Press the "Cancel" and allow a "Natural" release.
- Carefully, remove the lid and serve hot with the topping of the cheese.

Per Serving: Calories: 223; Total Fat: 15.2g; Saturated Fat: 9g; Protein: 8.5g; Carbs: 13.8g; Fiber: 3g; Sugar: 6.6g

Creamy Mushrooms

Serves: 4 / Preparation time: 15 minutes / Cooking time: 27 minutes

2½ cups fresh mushrooms, sliced

¼ cup plain yogurt

Salt and ground black pepper, to taste

½ cup unsweetened coconut milk

¾ teaspoon fresh ginger, grated

- In a Pyrex dish, mix together all the ingredients.
- With a piece of foil, cover the dish.
- Arrange a steamer trivet in the bottom of an Instant Pot Mini and pour 1 cup of the water.
- Place the Pyrex dish on top of the trivet.
- Secure the lid and turn to "Seal" position.
- Cook on "Manual" with "High Pressure" for about 25-27 minutes.
- Press the "Cancel" and allow a "Natural" release.
- Carefully, remove the lid and stir the mixture well.
- Serve hot.

Per Serving: Calories: 91; Total Fat: 7.5g; Saturated Fat: 6.5g; Protein: 3g; Carbs: 4.5g; Fiber: 1.2g; Sugar: 2.9g

Mushrooms with Zucchini

Serves: 4 / Preparation time: 15 minutes / Cooking time: 10 minutes

6-ounces sliced fresh mushrooms

1/2 cup white onion, chopped

1 garlic clove, minced

2 fresh zucchinis, cut into ½-inch slices

1 tbsp fresh basil leaves, chopped

1/2 tbsp olive oil

1/2 cup cream

1/2 cup cheddar cheese

1/2 cup feta cheese

Salt and ground black pepper, as required

½ (7-ounce) can sugar-free crushed tomatoes (with juice)

- Place olive oil in the Instant Pot and press "Sauté". Then, place the onion, mushrooms and garlic and sear for about 5 minutes.
- Stir in the basil, zucchinis, salt and black pepper and sear for about 2 minutes.
- Select the "Cancel" and spread tomatoes over the vegetables evenly.
- Secure the lid and turn to "Seal" position.
- Cook on "Manual" with "Low Pressure" for about 2 minutes.
- Press the "Cancel" and allow a "Natural" release.
- Carefully, remove the lid and serve immediately.

Per Serving: Calories: 114; Total Fat: 4g; Saturated Fat: 0.8g; Protein: 6.3g; Carbs: 16.7g; Fiber: 5.8g; Sugar: 9.7g

Spinach in Tomato Sauce

Serves: 4 / Preparation time: 15 minutes / Cooking time: 13 minutes

2 tablespoons olive oil

1 tablespoon garlic, minced

8 cups fresh spinach, chopped

½ cup tomato puree

¾ cup vegetable broth

1 medium onion, chopped

½ teaspoon red pepper flakes, crushed

1 cup tomatoes, chopped

½ cup white wine

Salt, to taste

- Add the oil in an Instant Pot Mini and select "Sauté". Now, add the onion and cook for about 3-4 minutes.
- Add the garlic and red pepper flakes and cook for about 1 minute.
- Add the spinach and cook for about 2 minutes.
- Press the "Cancel" and stir in the remaining ingredients.
- Secure the lid and turn to "Seal" position.
- Cook on "Manual" with "High Pressure" for about 6 minutes.
- Press the "Cancel" and allow a "Quick" release.
- Carefully, remove the lid and serve warm.

Per Serving: Calories: 140; Total Fat: 7.7g; Saturated Fat: 1.1g; Protein: 4g; Carbs: 11.1g; Fiber: 3.1g; Sugar: 4g

Garlicky Bok Choy

Serves: 4 / Preparation time: 15 minutes / Cooking time: 7 minutes

1 bunch bok choy, trimmed

2 tablespoons oyster sauce

2 garlic cloves, minced

Salt and ground black pepper, to taste

1 cup water

2 tablespoons olive oil

1/8 teaspoon red pepper flakes, crushed

- In the pot of an Instant Pot Mini, place the stems of bok choy and top with the water and oyster sauce, followed by the green part of bok choy.
- Secure the lid and turn to "Seal" position.
- Cook on "Manual" with "High Pressure" for about 7 minutes.
- Press the "Cancel" and allow a "Quick" release.
- Meanwhile, in a small frying pan, heat the oil over medium heat and sauté the garlic and red pepper flakes for about 1 minute.
- Mix in the salt and black pepper and immediately remove from the heat.
- Carefully, remove the lid and transfer the bok choy stems and leaves into a large serving bowl with some cooking liquid.
- Place the garlic mixture over the bok choy and gently, stir to combine.
- Serve immediately.

Per Serving: Calories: 91; Total Fat: 7.4g; Saturated Fat: 1.1g; Protein: 3.3g; Carbs: 5.3g; Fiber: 2.2g; Sugar: 2.5g

Kale with Carrots

Serves: 4 / Preparation time: 15 minutes / Cooking time: 14 minutes

1 tablespoon olive oil

2 medium carrots, peeled and cut into ½-inch slices

1 small onion, chopped   4 garlic cloves, minced

10 ounces fresh kale, tough ends removed and chopped

½ cup vegetable broth   Salt and ground black pepper, to taste

1 tablespoon fresh lemon juice   Pinch of red pepper flakes

- Add the oil in an Instant Pot Mini and select "Sauté". Now, add the carrot and onion and cook for about 5 minutes.
- Add the garlic and cook for about 1 minute.
- Press the "Cancel" and stir in the kale, broth, salt and black pepper.
- Secure the lid and turn to "Seal" position.
- Cook on "Manual" with "High Pressure" for about 8 minutes.
- Press the "Cancel" and allow a "Quick" release.
- Carefully, remove the lid and mix in the lemon juice.
- Serve with the sprinkling of red pepper flakes.

Per Serving: Calories: 95; Total Fat: 0.6g; Saturated Fat: 0.6g; Protein: 3.4g; Carbs: 13.2g; Fiber: 2.3g; Sugar: 2.5g

Stuffed Eggplants

Serves: 4 / Preparation time: 20 minutes / Cooking time: 8 minutes

For Stuffing Spices

1 teaspoon coriander seeds
½ teaspoon mustard seeds
2 tablespoons coconut shreds
2 garlic cloves, chopped
1 hot green chile, chopped
½ teaspoon cayenne pepper
½ teaspoon ground cardamom
Salt, as required
1-2 teaspoons water

½ teaspoon cumin seeds
2-3 tablespoons chickpea flour
2 tablespoons peanuts, chopped
1 teaspoon fresh ginger, chopped
½ teaspoon jaggery
½ teaspoon ground turmeric
Pinch of ground cinnamon
1 teaspoon fresh lemon juice

For Curry

4 baby eggplants
Salt, to taste
2 tablespoons fresh cilantro, chopped

1 cup water
½ teaspoon garam masala powder

- Select "Sauté" of an Instant Pot Mini. Now, add the seeds and cook for about 1 minute, stirring continuously.
- Add the chickpea flour and cook for about 1 minute, stirring continuously.
- Add the coconut and peanuts and cook for about 1 minute, stirring continuously.
- Press the "Cancel" and transfer the peanut mixture into a spice grinder.
- Then, grind the peanut mixture until roughly ground.
- In a bowl, add the peanut mixture, garlic, ginger, chile, jaggery, ground spices, lemon juice and water and mix until a coarse paste is formed.
- For curry: with a sharp knife, make cross cuts on each eggplant, not all the way through.
- Carefully, fill the stuffing into the cross cut.
- In the pot of Instant Pot Mini, place the eggplants in a single later, cut side up.
- Carefully, add water and salt around the eggplants.
- Secure the lid and turn to "Seal" position.
- Cook on "Manual" with "High Pressure" for about 4-5 minutes.
- Press the "Cancel" and allow a "Natural" release.
- Carefully, remove the lid and sprinkle with the garam masala.
- Serve hot with the garnishing of cilantro.

Per Serving: Calories: 92; Total Fat: 3.8g; Saturated Fat: 1.1g; Protein: 3.9g; Carbs: 12.7g; Fiber: 4.2g; Sugar: 4g

Stuffed Spicy Potatoes

Serves: 4 / Preparation time: 20 minutes / Cooking time: 16 minutes

8-10 cashews

8 baby potatoes

1 large onion, chopped finely

1½ teaspoons fresh ginger, chopped finely

½ teaspoon ground turmeric

1 teaspoon garam masala powder

1 tablespoon fresh cilantro, chopped finely

¼ cup warm milk

2 tablespoons ghee

1½ teaspoons garlic, chopped finely

2 ripe red tomatoes, pureed

¾ tablespoon chili powder

Salt, as required

- In a small bowl, soak the cashews in the warm milk for about 10 minutes.
- Peel the potatoes and then, remove core from the top of each, reserving the carved-out pieces.
- Add the ghee in the Instant Pot Mini and select "Sauté". Now, add the onion and cook for about 2 minutes.
- Add garlic and ginger and cook for about 30 seconds.
- Add the reserved carved-out potato pieces, tomato paste and spices and cook for about 2 minutes.
- Press the "Cancel" and fill the carved potatoes with the cooked gravy.
- In the pot of Instant Pot, arrange the potatoes and add ½ cup of water.
- Secure the lid and turn to "Seal" position.
- Cook on "Manual" with "High Pressure" for about 8 minutes.
- Press the "Cancel" and allow a "Quick" release.
- Meanwhile, in a blender, add the cashews with milk and pulse until smooth.
- Carefully, remove the lid and select "Sauté".
- Stir in the cashew paste and cilantro and cook for about 2-3 minutes.
- Press the "Cancel" and serve hot.

Per Serving: Calories: 191; Total Fat: 11.2g; Saturated Fat: 5g; Protein: 4.2g; Carbs: 21.1g; Fiber: 4g; Sugar: 5.2g

Potatoes with Peas

Serves: 4 / Preparation time: 15 minutes / Cooking time: 10 minutes

2 tablespoons olive oil

1 medium onion, chopped finely

½ tablespoon fresh ginger, chopped finely

½ tablespoon garlic, chopped finely

1 green chili, sliced thinly

1 teaspoon cumin seeds

1 cup tomato puree

1 teaspoon garam masala powder

1 teaspoon ground coriander

½ teaspoon red chili powder

½ teaspoon ground turmeric

Salt, to taste

5 medium potatoes, peeled and chopped

1 cup fresh green peas, shelled

1 cup water

2 tablespoons fresh cream

2 tablespoons fresh cilantro, chopped

- Add the oil in an Instant Pot Mini and select "Sauté". Now, add the onion, ginger, garlic, green chili and cumin seeds and cook for about 4-5 minutes.
- Stir in the tomato puree and spices and cook for about 1-2 minutes.
- Press the "Cancel" and stir in the potatoes, peas and water.
- Secure the lid and turn to "Seal" position.
- Cook on "Manual" with "High Pressure" for about 3 minutes.
- Press the "Cancel" and allow a "Quick" release.
- Carefully, remove the lid and mix in the cream and cilantro
- Serve hot.

Per Serving: Calories: 283; Total Fat: 8.1g; Saturated Fat: 1.4g; Protein: 7.2g; Carbs: 48.5g; Fiber: 9.1g; Sugar: 8.9g

Peas with Cottage Cheese

Serves: 4 / Preparation time: 20 minutes / Cooking time: 17 minutes

2 tablespoons vegetable oil	1½ cups onions, chopped finely
1 tablespoon fresh ginger, minced	1 tablespoon garlic, minced
1 cup tomatoes, chopped finely	1 teaspoon garam masala powder
1 teaspoon cayenne pepper	1 teaspoon ground turmeric
Salt, to taste	¾ cup water, divided
12 ounces peas, shelled	1 cup cottage cheese, chopped
¼ cup heavy whipping cream	¼ cup fresh cilantro, chopped finely

- Add the oil in an Instant Pot Mini and select "Sauté". Now, add the onion and cook for about 2-3 minutes.
- Add the ginger and garlic and cook for about 1 minute.
- Press the "Cancel" and stir in the tomatoes, spices and ¼ cup of the water.
- Secure the lid and turn to "Seal" position.
- Cook on "Manual" with "High Pressure" for about 5 minutes.
- Press the "Cancel" and allow a "Quick" release.
- Press the "Cancel" and allow a "Natural" release for about 5 minutes and then allow a "Quick" release.
- Carefully, remove the lid and select "Sauté".
- Stir in the peas, cottage cheese, whipping cream and remaining water and cook for about 5-8 minutes, stirring occasionally.
- Press the "Cancel" and serve hot with the garnishing of cilantro.

Per Serving: Calories: 243; Total Fat: 11.4g; Saturated Fat: 3.9g; Protein: 13.8g; Carbs: 22.6g; Fiber: 6.3g; Sugar: 8.2g

Jackfruit Curry

Serves: 3 / Preparation time: 15 minutes / Cooking time: 18 minutes

1 teaspoon canola oil

½ teaspoon nigella seeds

2 dried red chilies

1 small onion, chopped

5 garlic cloves, chopped

½ teaspoon ground turmeric

1½ cups tomato puree

1 (20-ounce) can green Jackfruit, drained and rinsed

1-1½ cups water

½ teaspoon cumin seeds

½ teaspoon mustard seeds

2 bay leaves

1 teaspoon fresh ginger, chopped

1 teaspoon ground coriander

Salt and ground black pepper, to taste

- Add the oil in an Instant Pot Mini and select "Sauté". Now, add all the seeds and cook for about 1 minute, stirring continuously.
- Add the red chilies and bay leaves cook for 20-30 seconds, stirring continuously.
- Add the onion, ginger, garlic and a pinch of salt and cook for about 5-6 minutes, stirring occasionally.
- Add the spices and tomato puree and cook for about 2 minutes.
- Press the "Cancel" and stir in the jackfruit and water.
- Secure the lid and turn to "Seal" position.
- Cook on "Manual" with "High Pressure" for about 8 minutes.
- Press the "Cancel" and allow a "Natural" release.
- Carefully, remove the lid and serve hot.

Per Serving: Calories: 410; Total Fat: 2.2g; Saturated Fat: 0.2g; Protein: 3g; Carbs: 16.3g; Fiber: 4.7g; Sugar: 59.4g

Cauliflower Rice

Serves: 4 / Preparation time: 15 minutes / Cooking time: 13 minutes

1 medium head cauliflower, cut into large pieces

2 tablespoon olive oil

¼ teaspoon ground cumin

¼ teaspoon ground turmeric

2 tablespoons fresh parsley, chopped

½ teaspoon dried thyme

¼ teaspoon paprika

Salt, to taste

- In the bottom of an Instant Pot Mini, arrange a steamer trivet and pour 1 cup of the water.
- Place the cauliflower pieces on top of the trivet.
- Secure the lid and turn to "Seal" position.
- Cook on "Manual" with "High Pressure" for about 10 minutes.
- Press the "Cancel" and allow a "Quick" release.
- Carefully, remove the lid and transfer the cauliflower onto a plate.
- Remove water from the pot and with paper towels, pat dry it.
- Add the oil in an Instant Pot Mini and select "Sauté". Now, add the cooked cauliflower and with a spoon, break into smaller chunks.
- Add the spices and cook for about 1-2 minutes.
- Press the "Cancel" and serve hot with the garnishing of parsley.

Per Serving: Calories: 79; Total Fat: 7.2g; Saturated Fat: 1g; Protein: 1.4g; Carbs: 3.9g; Fiber: 1.9g; Sugar: 1.6g

THE "DIRTY DOZEN" AND "CLEAN 15"

Every year, the Environmental Working Group releases a list of the produce with the most pesticide residue (Dirty Dozen) and a list of the ones with the least **chance of having residue (Clean 15). It's based on analysis from the U.S.** Department of Agriculture Pesticide Data Program report.

The Environmental Working Group found that 70% of the 48 types of produce tested had residues of at least one type of pesticide. In total there were 178 different pesticides and pesticide breakdown products. This residue can stay on veggies and fruit even after they are washed and peeled. All pesticides are toxic to humans and consuming them can cause damage to the nervous system, reproductive system, cancer, a weakened immune system, and more. Women who are pregnant can expose their unborn children to toxins through their diet, and continued exposure to pesticides can affect their development.

This info can help you choose the best fruits and veggies, as well as which ones you should always try to buy organic.

The Dirty Dozen

- Strawberries
- Spinach
- Nectarines
- Apples
- Peaches
- Celery
- Grapes
- Pears
- Cherries
- Tomatoes
- Sweet bell peppers
- Potatoes

The Clean 15

- Sweet corn
- Avocados
- Pineapples
- Cabbage
- Onions
- Frozen sweet peas
- Papayas
- Asparagus
- Mangoes
- Eggplant
- Honeydew
- Kiwi
- Cantaloupe
- Cauliflower
- Grapefruit

MEASUREMENT CONVERSION TABLES

Volume Equivalents (Dry)

US Standard	Metric (Approx.)
¼ teaspoon	1 ml
½ teaspoon	2 ml
1 teaspoon	5 ml
1 tablespoon	15 ml
¼ cup	59 ml
½ cup	118 ml
1 cup	235 ml

Weight Equivalents

US Standard	Metric (Approx.)
½ ounce	15 g
1 ounce	30 g
2 ounces	60 g
4 ounces	115 g
8 ounces	225 g
12 ounces	340 g
16 oz or 1 lb	455 g

Volume Equivalents (Liquid)

US Standard	US Standard (ounces)	Metric (Approx.)
2 tablespoons	1 fl oz	30 ml
¼ cup	2 fl oz	60 ml
½ cup	4 fl oz	120 ml
1 cup	8 fl oz	240 ml
1 ½ cups	12 fl oz	355 ml
2 cups or 1 pint	16 fl oz	475 ml
4 cups or 1 quart	32 fl oz	1 L
1 gallon	128 fl oz	4 L

Oven Temperatures

Fahrenheit (F)	Celsius (C) (Approx)
250°F	120°C
300°F	150°C
325°F	165°C
350°F	180°C
375°F	190°C
400°F	200°C
425°F	220°C
450°F	230°C

INDEX

B

BBQ Pork Baby Back Ribs, 57
BBQ Pork Spare Ribs, 56
Beef & Carrot Curry, 70
Beef & Chickpeas Curry, 73
Beef & Mushroom Soup, 66
Beef & Tomato Curry, 71
Beef & Veggie Chili, 69
Beef & Veggie Stew, 67
Beef Lasagna, 85
Beef Meatballs Stew, 68
Beef with Bell Peppers, 76
Beef with Broccoli, 75
Beef with Green Beans, 74
Beef with Tuna Sauce, 80
Beer Braised Pulled Pork, 60
Beet Salad, 112
Buttered Crab Legs, 109

C

Calamari with Tomatoes, 106
Catfish Curry, 93
Cauliflower Rice, 125
Cheese Stuffed Beef Burgers, 87
Chicken & Chickpeas Soup, 21
Chicken & Corn Chili, 26
Chicken & Kale Soup, 19
Chicken & Mushroom Stew, 23
Chicken & Squash Soup, 20
Chicken & Tomato Curry, 27
Chicken & Veggie Chili, 25
Chicken & Veggie Curry, 28
Chicken with Olives, 32
Chicken with Pineapple, 31
Chicken with Salsa, 33
Chicken, Rice & Lentil Stew, 24
Citrus Salmon, 95
Clam Soup, 91
Cod Parcel, 102
Cod with Peas, 101
Cod with Tomatoes, 100
Coffee Braised Pulled Beef, 81
Creamy Chicken Soup, 18
Creamy Chicken Stew, 22

Creamy Mushrooms, 115
Creamy Pork Chops, 54
Creamy Potato Salad, 113
Creamy Shredded Chicken, 30

G

Garlicky Bok Choy, 118
Ground Beef with Cabbage & Rice, 83
Ground Beef with Peas, 82
Ground Beef with Veggies & Oats, 84
Ground Pork & Cabbage Soup, 44
Ground Pork & Green Beans Soup, 43

H

Haddock Soup, 90
Ham & Split Peas Soup, 46
Herbed Chicken Breasts, 34
Honey Glazed Steak, 77

J

Jackfruit Curry, 124

K

Kale with Carrots, 119

L

Lemony Mussels, 107
Lemony Pulled Pork, 61

M

Marinated Beef Curry, 72
Mushrooms with Zucchini, 116

O

Onion Soup, 114

P

Peas with Cottage Cheese, 123
Pork & Bok Choy Soup, 42
Pork & Corn Stew, 47
Pork & Veggie Stew, 45
Pork Chops with Apple, 55
Pork Curry, 50
Pork Ribs in Mustard Sauce, 51
Pork Sausage & Veggie Stew, 48

Pork Sausage with Potato Mash, 63
Pork Sausage with Quinoa, 62
Pork Tenderloin with Fruit, 58
Pork Vindaloo, 49
Pork with Mushrooms, 53
Pork with Pineapple, 52
Potatoes with Peas, 122

R

Roasted Whole Chicken, 37

S

Salmon Casserole, 98
Salmon Curry, 94
Salmon in Creamy Sauce, 97
Salmon in Green Sauce, 96
Seafood Stew, 92
Shrimp with Green Beans, 104
Shrimp with Potatoes, 103
Shrimp with Rice, 105
Spicy Chicken Thighs, 35
Spicy Pork Butt, 59
Spinach in Tomato Sauce, 117
Steak in Orange Sauce, 78
Steak with Salsa, 79
Steamed Lobster Tails, 108
Stuffed Eggplants, 120
Stuffed Spicy Potatoes, 121
Sweet & Sour Chicken Thighs, 36
Sweet & Sour Mahi-Mahi, 99
Sweet & Sour Meatballs, 86
Sweet & Sour Shredded Chicken, 29

T

Turkey Stuffed Bell Peppers, 39
Turkey with Quinoa & Chickpeas, 38

Made in the USA
Middletown, DE
19 August 2019